BBC

Speakout
3RD EDITION

A2+

Workbook

Pearson Education Limited
KAO Two
KAO Park
Hockham Way
Harlow, Essex
CM17 9SR
England
and Associated Companies throughout the world.

pearsonenglish.com/speakout3e

© Pearson Education Limited 2023

All rights reserved; no part of this publication may be reproduced, stored in a retrieval system, or transmitted in any form or by any means, electronic, mechanical, photocopying, recording, or otherwise without the prior written permission of the Publishers.

First published 2023
Seventh impression 2024

ISBN: 978-1-292-40736-4

Set in BBC Reith Sans

Printed and bound by CPI Group (UK) Ltd, Croydon CR0 4YY

Acknowledgements
Written by Lindsay Warwick

Image Credit(s):
123RF.com: Cathy Yeulet 38, limagesstudio 59, mangostar 13, Michael Simons 9, stockbroker 41, victorass88 52; **Getty Images:** agrobacter/E+ 31, ajr_images/iStock 38, Alan Thornton/The Image Bank 67, alvarez/E+ 37, Amer Dzuderija/EyeEm 11, Andrea Pistolesi/Stone 25, AzmanL/E+ 9, BraunS/E+ 19, Carlos Barquero 51, Compassionate Eye Foundation/Steve Smith/DigitalVision 38, Dima Berlin/iStock 12, DisobeyArt/iStock 9, Flashpop/DigitalVision 52, FluxFactory/E+ 23, FreshSplash/E+ 13, Johner Images 35, Jupiterimages/Stockbyte 21, Justin Paget/DigitalVision 47, Luis Alvarez/DigitalVision 52, Maskot 9, Maskot/DigitalVision 9, Michael Truelove/Image Source 7, Mike Harrington/DigitalVision 44, Nicolas Maeterlinck/AFP 43, Peter Cade/Stone 38, powerofforever/E+ 21, Rakratchada Torsap/EyeEm 29, Robin Skjoldborg/DigitalVision 13, svetikd/E+ 49, Tim Robberts/DigitalVision 5, Westend61 34, wonry/E+ 53, Xavier Lorenzo 6, Yoshiyoshi Hirokawa/DigitalVision 38, Yukinori Hasumi 7; **Pearson Education Ltd:** Gareth Boden 9; **Shutterstock:** Dajra 36, Mikhail Bakunovich 9, ostill 52, racorn 13

Cover Images:
Front: **Getty Images:** adamkaz, Riska, Westend61

CONTENTS

LESSON	VOCABULARY	GRAMMAR	PRONUNCIATION
1A pp4–5	common verbs; everyday activities	questions	intonation in questions
1B pp6–7	job phrases; jobs	present simple and continuous	linking: *are*
1C | 1D pp8–9	feelings	verb + *-ing* form	stress in short phrases
2A pp10–11	animals	past simple and continuous	weak forms: *was*, *were*
2B pp12–13	air travel; at the airport	definite article: *the*	strong and weak forms: *the*
2C | 2D pp14–15	actions	*all*, *some*, *both*, *none of them*	intonation in offers
REVIEW 1–2 pp16–17			
3A pp18–19	knowing, understanding and thinking; school and university subjects	*have to*, *don't have to*, *can't*	connected speech: *have to*
3B pp20–21	positive adjectives	subject and object questions	word stress in adjectives
3C | 3D pp22–23	location, position and movement	*had to*, *didn't have to*, *couldn't*	intonation in short questions
4A pp24–25	irregular past participles	present perfect simple (1)	irregular past participles
4B pp26–27	travel; travel phrases	comparatives and superlatives	sentence stress
4C | 4D pp28–29	giving gifts	verbs of sensation + adjective or *like*	intonation to show interest
REVIEW 3–4 pp30–31			
5A pp32–33	money and value	possessive pronouns, *whose*, *this/that*, *there/then*	sounds /s/ and /z/
5B pp34–35	countable and uncountable nouns	quantifiers	weak forms in quantifiers
5C | 5D pp36–37	common adjectives	verbs with two objects	phrasing
6A pp38–39	sports collocations (*play*, *do*, *go*)	adverbs of frequency and manner	sentence stress: modifiers with adverbs
6B pp40–41	actions; physical actions	present perfect simple (2)	weak and strong forms: *have*, *has*
6C | 6D pp42–43	health and illness; the body and symptoms	*be* + adjective + *to* infinitive	connected speech: final *-t* and *-d*
REVIEW 5–6 pp44–45			
7A pp46–47	going out and staying in	present continuous with future reference; other future forms	linking /j/, /w/ and /r/
7B pp48–49	eating out and eating in; containers	indefinite pronouns: *someone*, *nothing*, *anywhere*, etc.	sentence stress with indefinite pronouns
7C | 7D pp50–51	permission	adverbial and prepositional phrases	polite intonation when asking permission
8A pp52–53	change	*will* for predictions	contractions: *'ll* and *won't*
8B pp54–55	attitudes	first conditional	linking in conditionals
8C | 8D pp56–57	the environment	word building: nouns to adjectives	intonation in question tags
REVIEW 7–8 pp58–59			

CUMULATIVE REVIEW 1–4 pp60–61	CUMULATIVE REVIEW 5–8 pp62–63	CUMULATIVE REVIEW 1–8 pp64–67
AUDIOSCRIPTS pp68–77		**ANSWER KEY** pp78–96

Lesson 1A

GRAMMAR | questions
VOCABULARY | common verbs; everyday activities
PRONUNCIATION | intonation in questions

VOCABULARY

common verbs

1 Choose the correct word or phrase to complete the sentences.
1 Slow, quiet music helps me .... to sleep.
  a go   b cry   c join
2 I want to .... a sports club.
  a hide   b join   c pack
3 Are you .... for a taxi?
  a waiting   b waking up   c hiding
4 My best friend now lives abroad and I really .... him.
  a cry   b wait   c miss
5 We need to .... a bag for our trip away.
  a pack   b miss   c hide
6 I .... my key behind a book so no one can find it.
  a hide   b pack   c lock

everyday activities

2A Match the sentence beginnings (1–6) with the endings (a–f).
1 It's dark. Let's switch   a my teeth and go to bed.
2 I didn't get   b all the windows.
3 I think I need to pack   c the lights on.
4 Let's do   d the washing up.
5 I'm going to brush   e some clothes in a bag.
6 It's cold. Let's shut   f dressed until 11 a.m.

B Complete the blog post with the words in the box.

> away brush do dressed
> dry lock shut switch

A life of habits

My life is different to most people's. I wake up at 6 p.m. I get up and have a shower. I take my clothes out of the cupboard and I get ¹............... . I ²............... my hair so it's not wet. I go and eat dinner with my family. I ³............... the washing up. I dry the dishes and put them ⁴............... in the cupboard. I ⁵............... my teeth. Then, I go to work. I work nights, from 10 p.m. to 6 a.m. I get home at 7 a.m. That's when my family has breakfast. After they go to work, I watch some TV. At about 10 a.m, I ⁶............... any open windows, take out my key and ⁷............... the door. I ⁸............... off any lights and go to bed!

GRAMMAR

questions

3A Choose the correct word or phrase to complete the sentences.
1 .... drink do you want – water or juice?
  a What kind   b Which   c How much
2 .... is our first meeting this morning?
  a When   b Who   c Why
3 Who .... that man over there?
  a does   b is   c do
4 .... do you do in your free time?
  a How   b What   c Which sort
5 .... you live here?
  a Are   b Is   c Do
6 .... do you travel to college?
  a How many   b How much   c How far

B Complete each question with one word.
1 A: .... do you play football?
   B: I play at the local sports centre.
2 A: When .... your birthday?
   B: It's on the 12th July.
3 A: What kind .... music do you like?
   B: I like all kinds.
4 A: .... do you ride a bike to work?
   B: Because it's cheaper than driving.
5 A: .... you got any sisters?
   B: Yes, I've got one.
6 A: How many children .... you have?
   B: I have three – two daughters and a son.
7 A: How .... is your home from here?
   B: It's about three kilometres.
8 A: .... colour do you prefer, blue or green?
   B: Green. It makes me think of trees.

PRONUNCIATION

4A **intonation in questions** | Do the speakers' voices rise (R) or fall (F) at the end of each question?
1 Who's your closest friend?
2 What colour are his eyes?
3 Does Ben live on his own?
4 Do you like chocolate cake?
5 How can I help you?
6 Do you ever play volleyball?

B 🔊 1.01 | Listen and check.

READING

5 Read the article. Choose the correct words to complete the sentences.

Mark and Hanna are ¹**friends / married**. Their lives are very ²**different / similar**.

6A Choose the things that are the same for both Mark and Hanna.

1. birthday
2. place of birth
3. primary school
4. secondary school
5. job
6. type of home now
7. hobby

B Complete the sentences with a word or year.

1. Hanna's date of birth is 26 April ....
2. Mark was born in ....
3. Hanna arrived in London when she was .... years old.
4. After secondary school, Mark got a job in a ....
5. Hanna went to university in ....
6. Mark and Hanna studied .... at university.
7. Mark and Hanna studied at university for .... years.
8. Mark and Hanna both live on the .... floor of their buildings.
9. Mark and Hanna met at a ....
10. Devon is a friend of Hanna's ....

C Who said these things, Mark (M) or Hanna (H)?

1. 'Cooking food for customers in the summer is hot!'
2. 'I really enjoyed spending time in my home country.'
3. 'I love working with students who are over 18. They're always really interested in my lessons.'
4. 'It was good to go to a university close to home. I could still enjoy my mum's cooking!'
5. 'One day, I want to live in an apartment on my own.'

New friends

Mark and Hanna are friends. They have a lot in common, and both went to the same school when they were very young. So why did they only become friends last month?

They were both born on 26th April. Mark was born in 1997 in London in the UK. Hanna was born in Amsterdam two years later. When Hanna was three, her family moved to the UK, to a house just ten minutes from Mark's home. They both went to Newbrook Primary School but they don't remember each other. Mark went to a different secondary school from Hanna.

After they finished secondary school, they each waited for a year before they went to university to study art. Mark worked in a restaurant to get some money and then travelled around Europe. Hanna went to Amsterdam and stayed with her aunt and uncle. Mark studied in London. Hanna went to Glasgow. They studied art for three years. Then, they both decided to stay at university for another year to become teachers. Mark finished university two years before Hanna. He got a job as an art teacher at a secondary school in London. Two years later, Hanna returned to London and got a job as an art teacher at an adult education college.

Today, Mark and Hanna both live in West London, in apartments that are on the fifth floor. Hanna lives alone, but Mark lives with a friend from university. They both enjoy going to museums and art galleries in their free time. In fact, they met at a museum. Last month, they went to a museum at the same time. Mark went with his friend Devon. Devon also knows Hanna because he's a friend of her cousin. And so, because of Devon, Mark and Hanna finally became friends!

Lesson 1B

GRAMMAR | present simple and continuous
VOCABULARY | job phrases; jobs
PRONUNCIATION | linking: *are*

VOCABULARY

job phrases; jobs

1 Match the speakers (1–8) with the jobs (a–h).

1. I start work at 4 a.m. so the office looks good when people arrive at 8 a.m.
2. My group and I perform on stage. We often work with singers in theatres.
3. My manager couldn't do her job without me. I plan everything!
4. I love looking after animals and helping them to get better when they are ill.
5. My company makes clothes. I work on one of the machines.
6. Sometimes, I write a story in a few weeks. Sometimes, in a few years!
7. Teeth are important to people. Everyone wants a nice smile.
8. I love showing people around my city and explaining its history.

a author   e factory worker
b cleaner   f PA
c dancer   g tour guide
d dentist   h vet

2A Choose the correct word or phrase to complete the sentences.

1. It's the chef's _____ to manage the kitchen and make sure the food is good.
   a career   b job   c work
2. I decided to take the job and signed the _____.
   a contract   b pay   c interview
3. I work in the technology _____.
   a job   b industry   c career
4. I need more time to _____ my own business.
   a do   b sign   c develop
5. The _____ here is 20% higher than at other similar companies.
   a pay   b interview   c industry
6. I was happy when the manager of the company _____ me the job.
   a signed
   b developed
   c offered

B Complete the text with the words in the box.

> business   career   contract   industry
> interviews   job   offered   pay

I'm a scientist in the food ¹_____. My ²_____ started after I left university. I had ³_____ with six different food and drinks companies. Five of them didn't want me. One of them ⁴_____ me a job. It was a small company and so the ⁵_____ wasn't very high, but I knew I could learn there. I signed the ⁶_____ and started a week later. I was a tester so my ⁷_____ was to test the fruit juices. I was there for ten years. Then I left and spent time developing my own science ⁸_____. Ten people work for me now.

GRAMMAR

present simple and continuous

3A The sentences below have a mistake. Choose the best option to correct the mistake.

1. Kate <u>aren't liking</u> the taste of coffee very much.
   a isn't liking   b doesn't like   c don't like
2. I <u>am travelling</u> a lot in my job.
   a am travel   b don't travelling   c don't travel
3. We<u>'re enjoy</u> our holiday this week.
   a 're enjoying   b enjoy   c 's enjoying
4. I <u>thinking</u> your job is very important.
   a 'm thinking   b 'm think   c think

B Complete the phone conversation with the present simple or the present continuous form of the verbs in brackets.

A: Hi Bella! It's Giorgio. How are you? ¹_____ you _____ (work)?
B: No, not today.
A: But you ²_____ (work) on Fridays.
B: Yes, usually, but not today. Today, I ³_____ (sit) in a café next to the river.
A: Nice! ⁴_____ you _____ (have) lunch?
B: Yes. I usually make myself the same lunch every day, but today I wanted something different.
A: What ⁵_____ you usually _____ (make)?
B: A boring cheese sandwich.
A: So, what ⁶_____ you _____ (eat) today in the café?
B: Pasta. It's lovely. What are you doing?
A: I ⁷_____ (enjoy) a walk in the park!
B: Oh! Is Martin with you?
A: No, he ⁸_____ (have) lunch in the office.
B: ⁹_____ he usually _____ (eat) at his desk?
A: Yes and so do I. Usually, we ¹⁰_____ (not / have) time to go out, but I want to enjoy the sun.
B: Me too. It's a beautiful day!

PRONUNCIATION

4 🔊 **1.02 | linking: *are* |** Listen and complete the questions with the words you hear.
1 What .... today?
2 Why .... in here?
3 Who .... about?
4 What .... for?
5 Where .... now?

LISTENING

5 📄 🔊 **1.03 |** Listen to the recording. Choose the words in the text that are different from what you hear.

> People pay a Japanese man called Shoji Morimoto to go out with them, because they don't want to be alone. It can be to a restaurant, a party or a wedding. One person even paid him to say goodbye to them at a bus station when they left Tokyo to travel to a different city.

6A 🔊 **1.04 |** Listen to a news story. What is Marta Morales's job?
a She makes wedding dresses.
b She helps brides on their wedding day.
c She plans weddings for couples.

B 🔊 **1.04 |** Listen again. Are the statements True (T) or False (F)?
1 Some brides want someone at a wedding who is more fun than their friends.
2 Wedding guests always know that Marta is doing a job.
3 Marta first meets the bride on the wedding day.
4 Marta was surprised by the number of brides who want someone like her.
5 Marta always feels very excited at the end of a wedding day.

C 🔊 **1.04 |** Listen again and complete each sentence with a number or a word.
1 Marta gets paid £................ for each wedding.
2 In her job, Marta has to stop people from ....
3 Marta started her company .... years ago.
4 Marta worked in a .... before she started working with brides.
5 Marta usually feels .... when she returns home after a wedding.

WRITING

an informal email

7A Read the email. Choose the correct words or phrases to complete the sentences.
1 Jamie is in Canada for **a few months / a year**.
2 Jamie **works / doesn't work** eight hours a day.
3 Jamie lives **alone / with others**.
4 The place where Jamie is staying **is / isn't** small.
5 Jamie asks a question about **free time / work**.

> Hi!
>
> How are you? I'm living in Canada at the moment. I'm working as a ski instructor for the winter.
>
> ¹................ It's my first year here, but I love it! I start teaching at 9.45 a.m. and finish at 3.30 p.m. It's not a long day, but I get very tired. ²................
>
> I'm living in an apartment with two other teachers. The apartment's not big, but it's clean and comfortable. The other teachers are a lot of fun.
> ³................
>
> Anyway, what are you doing these days? ⁴................
> Are you doing the same job? ⁵................
>
> Jamie

B Complete the gaps in the email (1–5) with the sentences (a–e).
a That's because I'm teaching children!
b Write and let me know!
c One of them is teaching me to play the guitar.
d I'm in Banff.
e Are you living in the same place?

C You are going to reply to Jamie. Imagine you are in a different country doing one of the jobs in the box below, or a job of your choice. Make notes on the topics (1–4).

> dancer   English teacher at a summer school
> farm worker   tour guide

1 general information about your life
2 your working day
3 your living situation
4 questions you want to ask Jamie

D Write an email to Jamie. Tell him what you are doing. Use your ideas in Ex 7C to help you. Write 80–120 words.

Lesson 1C

HOW TO ... | encourage people
VOCABULARY | feelings
PRONUNCIATION | stress in short phrases

VOCABULARY

feelings

1 A Match the statements (1–8) with the feelings in the box.

> afraid   confident   interested   lonely
> pleased   positive   stressed   unhappy

1 I'm sure I can pass my driving test. I've had a lot of practice.
2 Bad things happen sometimes, but mostly things go well!
3 I don't like high places. I don't want to fall!
4 They offered me the job!
5 Moving to a new city is hard. I don't have anyone to talk to.
6 It's 4 p.m. and I have a lot of work to finish before I can go home.
7 The food arrived late and it wasn't what I ordered!
8 You lived in Mozambique? Wow, tell me all about it!

B Choose the correct word or phrase to complete the sentences.

1 I'm sorry you're **afraid** / **pleased** / **unhappy** with the room in your hotel.
2 Are you feeling **confident** / **interested** / **lonely** about your exam?
3 I'd like to try a dangerous sport, but I'm too **afraid** / **positive** / **stressed**!
4 I feel very **interested** / **lonely** / **positive** when I live on my own and no one comes to visit me.
5 I'm really **interested** / **pleased** / **positive** in learning more about these trees.
6 Eddie looks tired and **confident** / **pleased** / **stressed** today.

PRONUNCIATION

2 🔊 **1.05 | stress in short phrases |** Listen to the phrases and choose the word with the main stress (a or b).

1 It's fine, really.
   a fine   b really
2 You can do it!
   a can   b do
3 It looks great!
   a looks   b great
4 That's all right.
   a all   b right
5 What do you think?
   a you   b think
6 I know what you mean.
   a what   b mean

How to ...

encourage people

3 A 🔊 **1.06 |** Listen to the conversations (1–4). Are the statements True (T) or False (F)?

1 Someone is making some changes to their home.
2 Someone is running and wants to stop.
3 Someone didn't go to a meeting and is pleased about it.
4 A student wants to give a talk alone.

B 🔊 **1.06 |** Choose the correct words or phrases to complete the sentences. Then listen again and check.

1 Wow! It **looks** / **watches** great! **Kind** / **Nice** colour.
2 Well **do** / **done**! It's not an easy room to paint.
3 Just a few more minutes. You can do **it** / **them**.
4 You can! Go **on** / **off**! Keep running!
5 That's **all right** / **wrong**. I thought it was probably a bus problem.
6 **Don't** / **Not** worry. It's fine **really** / **very**. Just get a coffee and relax.
7 Not everyone likes giving presentations. I **understand** / **'m understanding**.
8 **That's** / **What's** a great idea! Yes, that's fine.

SPEAKING

4 A Complete the conversation with the words in the box.

> mean   that's   think   well   worry   you'll

A: My cousin wants me to introduce her and her new husband at their wedding dinner, but I've never talked in front of a lot of people before.
B: I know what you ¹_____. It's scary.
A: And my brother doesn't think I can do it.
B: Oh no! It's not important what he thinks. What do you ²_____?
A: I think I can do it.
B: Then don't ³_____. Give the introduction.
A: Can I practise with you now?
B: Yes, ⁴_____ a good idea!
A: OK, here goes … Ladies and Gentlemen, your attention, please. Please stand for the bride and groom, Mr and Mrs Brooks!
B: Oh, ⁵_____ done! That was great! Very clear and confident.
A: Thanks! So, shall I tell my cousin I can do it?
B: Yes, ⁶_____ be great!

B 🔊 **1.07 |** Listen and check.

C 🔊 **1.08 |** You are B in Ex 4A. Listen and speak after the beep. Record the conversation if you can.

D Listen to your recording and compare it to Ex 4B.

Speak anywhere   Go to the interactive speaking practice

8

Lesson 1D

GRAMMAR | verb + -ing form
LISTENING | likes and dislikes

GRAMMAR

verb + -ing form

1 Find and correct one mistake in each sentence.
   1 I enjoy to develop new skills.
   2 My friend hates makeing mistakes.
   3 We don't mind cook in the evenings.
   4 I enjoying begining a new hobby.
   5 I hate no sleeping well.
   6 I'd love having a different job one day.
   7 Karen doesn't mind to helping me with my work.
   8 We not like working on Friday afternoons.

2 Complete the article with the correct form of the verbs in brackets.

Love and hate

We asked our readers about things they love and hate at the same time. This is what some of them said.

Max_327
I really enjoy ¹_____ (dance) salsa, but salsa doesn't love me. I took lessons and broke my foot!

Kat
I love ² _____ (get) into a hot shower, but I hate ³ _____ (get) out of it. It feels so cold!

Enrico
I like ⁴ _____ (do) my job, but I'd like ⁵ _____ (have) more than one day off a week.

GinaB
I enjoy ⁶ _____ (visit) other countries but I hate ⁷ _____ (travel) there and back.

Adam99
I love ⁸ _____ (see) my sister once a year but I hate ⁹ _____ (say) goodbye to her. I miss her so much!

CarFan42
I don't mind ¹⁰ _____ (take) the bus or train but I'd hate ¹¹ _____ (use) them all the time. I love driving! The problem is that I hate ¹² _____ (be) on the roads with other drivers!

LISTENING

3 🔊 **1.09** | Listen to two friends. Complete the table with the things in the box.

baths in summer	hot chocolate
Monday mornings	public swimming pools
Sunday evenings	walking

Louis's dislikes	Millie's dislikes

4 🔊 **1.09** | Listen again. Choose the correct words.
   1 Louis doesn't like walking in **cold** / **warm** weather.
   2 Millie doesn't **mind** / **hates** losing games.
   3 Louis likes **arriving at** / **leaving** work late.
   4 Millie gets up **early** / **late** at the weekends.
   5 Louis prefers **baths** / **showers**.
   6 Millie **enjoys** / **doesn't like** hotel swimming pools.

5 📝 🔊 **1.10** | Listen to the recording. Write what you hear. You will hear the sentences only once.
   1 _____
   2 _____
   3 _____
   4 _____

Lesson 2A

GRAMMAR | past simple and continuous
VOCABULARY | animals
PRONUNCIATION | weak forms: *was, were*

VOCABULARY

animals

1 Choose the correct words to complete the sentences.
1 The cat's **feather / fur / trunk** was really soft.
2 There was a huge spider's **shell / web / wing** near the door.
3 Indian elephants have more hair on their **feathers / shell / skin** than African elephants.
4 All elephants use their **fur / trunk / wings** to drink.
5 The butterfly's **shells / webs / wings** were very colourful and pretty.
6 The tortoise was inside its **shell / skin / trunk**.
7 The bird flew away, but it left a few **feathers / tails / webs** behind.
8 The dog's **skin / tail / wing** was moving up and down fast. It was happy to see me!

2 Complete the definitions with the name of an animal.
1 a clever sea animal like a fish with a long grey nose: d..............
2 a black and yellow flying insect that makes honey: b..............
3 a small animal with long ears and soft fur and sometimes with a short white tail: r..............
4 a small green animal that lives near water and uses its long legs to jump: f..............
5 a large wild cat with a yellow and black body: t..............
6 a long thin animal with no legs that moves along the ground: s..............
7 an insect with four wings in pretty colours: b..............
8 a wild animal that looks like a dog and lives in groups: w..............

GRAMMAR

past simple and continuous

3 A The sentences below have a mistake. Choose the best option to correct the mistake.
1 We <u>drive</u> along the road when we saw a bear.
   a drove   **b** were driving   **c** were drove
2 I <u>call</u> for help when I saw the snake.
   a were calling   **b** called   **c** was calling
3 What <u>do you do</u> at 8 p.m. last night?
   a were you doing   **b** did you do   **c** were you do
4 We were swimming in the sea <u>which</u> we saw dolphins!
   a what   **b** while   **c** when

B Choose the correct words to complete the sentences.
1 Yesterday, I saw a fox in the street while I **walked / was walking** home.
2 Max **had / was having** goats when he lived in the country!
3 I'm sorry I **didn't hear / wasn't hearing** your call. I was listening to music.
4 My dog **made / was making** friends with a cat while we **walked / were walking** near the park.
5 When my neighbour **crossed / was crossing** the road, she **fell / was falling**, but she's fine now.
6 We **found / were finding** a lost dog and **took / was taking** it to the nearest vet's.

C Complete the conversation with the past simple or past continuous form of the verbs in brackets.
A: What ¹.............. (you / do) when I called you yesterday?
B: I ².............. (play) basketball in the park with some friends from work. Sorry I didn't answer.
A: That's all right. I called because something strange happened to me.
B: What?
A: Well, I ³.............. (walk) home from the supermarket when I ⁴.............. (hear) an unusual noise.
B: What was it?
A: It was a tiny fox. It ⁵.............. (lie) under a car. It was very afraid. I guess it couldn't find its mother.
B: Oh no! What ⁶.............. (you / do)?
A: I ⁷.............. (call) an animal rescue centre. They ⁸.............. (come) and took it away.
B: What happened after that?
A: I ⁹.............. (speak) to the vet at the centre this morning and she ¹⁰.............. (tell) me the fox was fine.
B: Oh, that's good.

PRONUNCIATION

4 A 🔊 2.01 | weak forms: *was, were* | Listen and complete the questions with the words you hear.
1 Where .... basketball?
2 Who .... to?
3 What .... you?
4 Who .... about?
5 Why .... a bus?
6 What .... early this morning?

B 🔊 2.01 | Listen again and repeat the sentences.

LISTENING

5 A 🔊 **2.02** | Listen to a story about a man from Scotland. Number the actions in the order you hear them (1–8).

- a He travelled to Amsterdam.
- b A cat ran to him.
- c He went to Bosnia and Herzegovina.
- d They travelled to thirty countries.
- e He cycled up a hill.
- f The cat got a special passport.
- g He took the cat to the vet.
- h He travelled to Greece.

B 🔊 **2.02** | Listen again and choose one option (a–c) to complete the sentences (1–6).

1 Dean travelled the world because he didn't enjoy
 - a where he lived.
 - b his manager.
 - c his work.
2 When Dean first saw Nala, he was travelling to
 - a Bosnia and Herzegovina.
 - b Italy.
 - c Montenegro.
3 Dean took Nala to the vet's office because he wanted to
 - a get Nala some medicine.
 - b find out about Nala's owner.
 - c check that Nala was well.
4 Dean says that Nala taught him to enjoy
 - a doing things more slowly.
 - b the sea more.
 - c being at home.
5 Dean can't go to some places with Nala because
 - a she can't get the right medicine.
 - b she doesn't have a pet passport.
 - c she can't stay in hotels.
6 People can learn most about Dean's story from
 - a his website.
 - b his social media page.
 - c his book.

C 📝 🔊 **2.03** | Listen to the recording. Write what you hear. You will hear the sentences only once.

1 ....
2 ....
3 ....
4 ....

WRITING

an animal story

6 A Read the story. Answer each question with one word from the story.

1 The writer rescued a ....
2 The writer rescued the animal from someone's ....
3 The home owner used his .... to open the door.

Animal rescue

Last year, I was out running when I saw a dog in the window of someone's house. ¹**Just then / First**, I saw smoke coming out of the house. There was a fire!

²**First / Later**, I used my phone to call the fire service. ³**Just then / Then**, I ran to the door of the building and I rang the doorbell. The owner wasn't at home, but he had a doorbell with a camera. He answered on his mobile phone. I explained the situation. The owner used his phone to open the front door.

The dog ran out into the street. It was very happy to see me! The fire service arrived quickly. ⁴**First, / Later**, the owner arrived. He was also very happy to see me!

B Read the story again and choose the correct time phrases to complete the sentences.

C Imagine you rescued a cat from a tree. Make notes on these things.

The beginning of the story
- where you were
- who you were with and what you were doing

The middle of the story
- where the cat was and why you needed to rescue it
- how you rescued it

The ending of the story
- what happened in the end
- how you felt

D Write your story with the title *Animal Rescue*. Write 80–120 words.

Lesson 2B

GRAMMAR | definite article: *the*
VOCABULARY | air travel; at the airport
PRONUNCIATION | strong and weak forms: *the*

VOCABULARY

air travel

1 Complete the blog post with the words in the box.

> arrival time   change   delay   due to arrive   fly out
> flight   land   made a reservation   take off

Ali Evans – 10 minutes ago

What a terrible start to my holiday in San Sebastián! The plan was to ¹............... from London and then ²............... in Madrid. Unfortunately, there was a problem with my first ³............... and it didn't ⁴............... until 15.30. That was a ⁵............... of over two hours. At the start of the flight, the pilot said that we were ⁶............... in Madrid at around 18.00, but the weather was terrible so we couldn't ⁷............... there. We went to a really small airport instead and then we had to take a bus to Madrid. My ⁸............... at Madrid airport was actually 20.30. It was too late to get a flight to San Sebastián.

I ⁹............... at a hotel in Madrid and there's where I am now. I'm on the 11.55 flight to San Sebastián tomorrow. Hope it's on time!

at the airport

2 A Choose the correct word or phrase to complete the sentences.

1 The man at the .... desk gave us our boarding passes.
   a check-in   **b** baggage   **c** customs
2 We went through .... where people checked our bags with X-ray machines.
   a passport control   **b** security   **c** departure
3 We went to the .... and waited to board the plane.
   a departure lounge   **b** customs   **c** check-in desk
4 We .... the plane and found our seats.
   a changed   **b** boarded   **c** got off
5 The woman at .... control looked at my photo and my face carefully.
   a lounge   **b** baggage   **c** passport
6 We walked through .... where people were checking luggage.
   a control   **b** arrivals   **c** customs

B Complete the advice with one word in each gap.

For first-time users of an airport

¹............... -in – show the staff your passport and ticket here. They take your large bags or suitcases and give you a ²............... pass.

³............... – here, you put your coat, wallet, keys in a tray and put it through the X-ray machine. Staff check you're not carrying anything dangerous.

Departure ⁴............... – go here to wait for your flight. Visit the shops and restaurants. Find your gate and ⁵............... your plane when it's ready.

Passport ⁶............... – show your passport to security staff after you ⁷............... off the plane in a different country.

⁸............... reclaim – collect your luggage here.

⁹............... – walk through this area. Staff might stop you and look in your luggage. Tell staff about any food or valuable items you have.

¹⁰............... hall – meet your friends here, and exit the airport to get a bus, train or taxi.

GRAMMAR

definite article: *the*

3 A Choose the correct words to complete the sentences.

1 Choose a seat, then put your bag on **seat / the seat**.
2 **Flight / The flight** to Barcelona is quite short.
3 It can take **time / the time** to find a cheap flight.
4 I'd love to visit **Sahara / the Sahara** Desert!
5 My flight leaves early **in morning / in the morning**.
6 Please meet me at **train station / the train station**.

B Complete the story with *the* or no article (–).

On a trip to ¹............... Sardinia, the Italian island, my friend and I rented a car. We wanted to go to a beach which ²............... tourists didn't usually visit and swim in ³............... Tyrrhenian Sea. So, we put all our bags in ⁴............... car. I put the destination into ⁵............... map on my phone and we started our journey. On the way, one of the roads was closed. The map gave us ⁶............... different choices and we chose the quickest one. That was a mistake, because ⁷............... road got worse and worse. It was scary! After an hour, we got to our destination. ⁸............... sea was beautiful and we were happy to be there, but it took us a long time to relax! In ⁹............... evening, we took a different route where the road was safer! We learnt that online maps aren't always right and ¹⁰............... safety is more important than time!

2B

PRONUNCIATION

4 🔊 2.04 | strong and weak forms: *the* | Listen to the sentences. Is *the* pronounced in its strong (S) or weak (W) form?

1 What's the name of your hotel?
2 This is the only morning flight.
3 I'd love to fly over the Andes.
4 We have to wait in the departure lounge.
5 My brother is in the arrivals hall.
6 The plane isn't very big.

READING

5 Read the article. Match each traveller (A–D) with the item they lost or forgot about (1–4).

1 passport
2 purse
3 mobile phone
4 ring

6A Read the article again. Are the statements True (T) or False (F)?

1 Darius asked others for help.
2 Darius's wife was upset about the ring.
3 Darius got a gift after his holiday.
4 Alice forgot something because she was helping someone else.
5 Alice thought it was funny when she found her phone.
6 Lucas found his passport when he was at the hotel.
7 Lucas's friends stayed with him in Mexico.
8 Lucas was happy when he found his passport.
9 Emi did something too fast.
10 Emi got the lost item back safely without any problems.

B Complete each sentence with one or two words from the article.

1 Darius was in the _____ on his own.
2 Alice wanted to use her phone to _____.
3 Alice's _____ was driving the car.
4 Lucas and his friends were in Tijuana for one _____.
5 Emi looked for her wallet when she was in the _____ of the airport.
6 Emi asked for help at the _____.

C Complete the plans with the name of a writer from Ex 5.

1 Next time, _____ is going to put everything in their car before they help others.
2 Next time, _____ is going to carefully check their bag when they can't find something.
3 Next time, _____ is going to check they have everything at the end of a flight.
4 Next time, _____ is going to take off one important thing before going swimming.

Travelling abroad: lost and (sometimes) found

Losing something on holiday is never fun. Here, four people tell us their stories about losing something abroad.

A Darius

One morning, on holiday with my wife, I went down to the pool alone. While I was swimming, I saw that my wedding ring wasn't on my finger. It was in the water! I asked people around me to look for it but none of us could find it. I was afraid to tell my wife, but she was fine about it. She bought me a new ring when we got home.

B Alice

My family and I were staying at a house in Florida. One morning, I put my phone on top of the car while I was putting my youngest child in his car seat. Then I got into the car and we drove off. Later, I wanted to take photos, but I couldn't find my phone anywhere. I looked in every bag, but it wasn't there! We found it when my husband drove over it. He was parking the car in front of our house and he didn't see it. It was completely broken. I was very upset about it at the time, but we can all laugh about it now.

C Lucas

I was in Mexico with some friends. We had a fantastic week in Tijuana. On our last day, we left the hotel and got in the car to go home. When we got to security at the border between Mexico and the USA, I couldn't find my passport. We went back to the hotel, but it wasn't there. I couldn't believe it! My friends had jobs to go to so they went home. I went to the US Embassy in Tijuana to get a new passport. It took two days. I wasn't pleased, but I felt worse when I got home and found my lost passport at the bottom of my bag.

D Emi

I was so excited when I landed in Paris that I got off the plane very quickly. In the arrivals hall, I saw that my purse wasn't in my bag. It was on my seat on the plane! I went to the airline desk and told them the problem. After an hour, someone brought me my purse. I was very pleased!

Lesson 2C

HOW TO ... | make and accept offers
VOCABULARY | actions
PRONUNCIATION | intonation in offers

VOCABULARY

actions

1 A Choose the correct word to complete the sentences.

1 We should make a .... of all these good ideas.
   a look   b note   c gift
2 It's kind to .... the door open for people.
   a hold   b carry   c take
3 I'll .... your suitcase to the car for you.
   a carry   b hold   c make
4 I always .... my son's hand when we're out.
   a bring   b carry   c hold
5 Let's take a .... at the new art shop.
   a hold   b look   c time
6 Here, I've .... you all some coffee.
   a held   b taken   c brought

B Complete the email with the words in the box.

answered (x2)   brought   cancelled
carried   made   take

Sorry I didn't reply earlier. As you know, I'm a PA and I've had a really busy day. I didn't even have time to ¹............... a break. My manager wasn't feeling well, so I ²............... all her appointments for the day. Then I ³............... all her emails. Next, I went out and ⁴............... back some flowers for her. I ⁵............... a tray with some soup to her office for lunch and then I ⁶............... lots of new appointments for her for the next week. During all that time, I ⁷............... the phone when it rang. And it rang a lot!

How to ...

make and accept offers

2 A 2.05 | Listen to the conversations (1–3). Choose the correct option (a or b).

1 The girl offers to help her friend
   a clean the house.
   b do her homework.
2 The woman offers to
   a cancel the man's appointment.
   b change the man's appointment.
3 The man offers to talk to
   a another student.
   b a colleague about her work.

B 2.06 | Put the words in the correct order to make sentences. Then listen and check.

1 to help / want me / you? / you / Do
2 great. / Yes, / would be / please. / That
3 do / I / washing up. / can / the
4 these cups / put / kitchen. / I'll / in the / all
5 it? / want me / you / cancel / Do / to
6 the one / book / the 24th? / Shall / on / I
7 email you / want me / the information? / Do / to / you
8 I'm / you, / OK. / Thank / but
9 her? / I / talk / Shall / to
10 you. / of / That's / kind
11 talk to / Let / first. / him / me
12 a / help. / great / OK, / that's

PRONUNCIATION

3 2.07 | intonation in offers | Listen and choose the offers that sound polite.

1 Let me carry your bags for you.
2 Shall I open a window?
3 I can take you to work.
4 Do you want us to help you?
5 Let me answer the email.
6 I'll hold the door open.

SPEAKING

4 A Complete the conversation with the words in the box.

but   can   good   let   go   shall   want

A: My sister and her children are coming for dinner tomorrow.
B: Oh, right. ¹............... I cook some pasta for us all?
A: That would be great.
B: I ²............... make a cake, too.
A: That's ³............... of you. Lucas and Carla love your lemon cake.
B: I know!
A: I can ⁴............... to the supermarket later and get everything we need.
B: Do you ⁵............... me to come with you?
A: Thank you, ⁶............... I'm OK. I don't need to get a lot.
B: ⁷............... me come with you. I can carry the bags to the car.
A: OK. That's fine with me!

B 2.08 | Listen and check.

C 2.09 | You are B in Ex 4A. Listen and speak after the beep. Record the conversation if you can.

D Listen to your recording and compare it to Ex 4B.

14

Speak anywhere   Go to the interactive speaking practice

Lesson 2D

GRAMMAR | *all, some, both, none of them*
READING | managing stress

GRAMMAR

all, some, both, none of them

1 Match the sentence beginnings (1–6) with the endings (a–f).

1 I want to speak to Nina and Sharif, but
2 We invited all our friends for dinner, but
3 Our manager asked the team to work late and
4 We planted some pretty flowers and
5 I went on holiday alone because
6 She laughed when she saw her two children because

a all of us agreed.
b two of them couldn't come.
c one of them had pen all over his face!
d none of my friends could afford the trip.
e both of them are away.
f most of them are still alive.

2 Complete the sentences with one word in each gap.

1 We wanted to get a coffee, but .... of us had any money.
2 I've got two brothers. .... of them are older than me. I'm the youngest.
3 Most of our meetings are online. Two of .... are in the office.
4 Please be on time. Some of .... usually come early, but most of you are late!
5 Most of .... people in my family live around here.
6 We .... want to have fun and enjoy the weekend. Every one of us.

READING

3 A Read the article. How many suggestions does it make for managing stress?

a three   b five   c seven

B Read the article again. Choose the correct words to complete the sentences.

1 The writer says everyday stressful situations are **small / big**.
2 She suggests we can **always / sometimes** leave a stressful situation.
3 She suggests **turning off phones / leaving phones in another room**.
4 We should exercise **regularly / when we're stressed**.
5 She says that it's **bad / good** to forget the time when doing a hobby.
6 She suggests **talking / not talking** about our stress.
7 She says we **always / don't always** need to talk to friends and family.
8 She believes **different / the same** ideas help different people.

4 Complete each sentence with one word from the article.

1 The writer says it's stressful when you can't talk to a .... person at the bank.
2 The writer says that university students can't just leave a ....
3 The writer suggests that for exercise, we should .... every day.
4 The writer believes that a hobby can help to .... off stress.
5 The writer suggests we meet new people by finding a .... to join.

What to do when you're stressed

Most days, we find ourselves in a stressful situation. Maybe we're late for work and every traffic light on the road turns red. Or we have a question about our bank account, but we can't seem to speak to a real person when we call. These are not huge problems, but when lots of things like this happen together, they can feel huge and we become really stressed. So, what should we do?

When we're in a really stressful situation, we can walk away and go to a different place. It's not always possible, of course. We can't always walk out of a business meeting or a university lecture. But these days, we use our phones or computers a lot to communicate with people for work or with friends and family. When the stress is coming from our phones and computers – maybe someone keeps emailing us or calling us or we can't get an app to work – we can switch them off. That's similar to leaving a room.

Regular exercise is good for stress. This doesn't mean we have to get up and run fast and far. A walk is enough to help us clear our heads. It's also really good for our general health, too, so we should all make time for a daily walk in our lives. We should also try to do something we enjoy every day. Baking? Video games? Drawing? It doesn't matter what it is. When we focus on something we like, we forget about the time. That's often good for us. It can help to switch off some of our stress.

Perhaps the most important thing is to talk to other people about how we feel. When we hold our stress inside, it can make us feel worse. Talk to friends, family, a doctor or join a club and meet new people and talk to them.

Stress is a part of life, but there are different ways to manage it. We just need to find what works for us.

1–2 REVIEW

GRAMMAR

1 A Put the words in the correct order to make questions.
1. this T-shirt / much / cost / does / How
2. sort of / you / What / do / work / do?
3. parents / Where / today / your / are
4. from here? / is / How / your house / far
5. here? / you / Do / sit / want to
6. ideas? / have / you / Do / good / any

B Use the prompts to make questions.
1. What / be / your date of birth?
2. you / like / this song?
3. How many bikes / Leo / have?
4. Tom and Luke / brothers?
5. What kind / videos / you / like?
6. How old / your cat?

2 Choose the correct words to complete the text.

My sister and I are very different but we're good friends. Kerry ¹**is living / lives** in Australia at the moment. She ²**'s working / works** at a technology company there for a few months. I don't understand what she does exactly, but she ³**'s liking / likes** it. She ⁴**'s working / works** too much in every job she does, but her pay is always good. She ⁵**'s enjoying / enjoys** sport and she ⁶**'s playing / plays** a lot of beach volleyball these days.

As for me, I'm still in the same house I grew up in! I'm an actor. I love my job, too, but I ⁷**'m not working / don't work** every day and I don't make a lot of money.

3 Complete the sentences with the correct form of the verbs in the box.

| do go have join make swim travel work |

1. I love .... out with friends on a Friday night.
2. I don't mind .... at the shop on Saturdays.
3. Alex would love .... around India.
4. We really enjoy .... our own pizzas.
5. I don't know anyone who likes .... the washing up!
6. Dinah loves .... in the sea.
7. I'd hate .... a job in an office.
8. Paul likes .... different sports clubs.

4 Correct the underlined mistake in each sentence.
1. A bird tried to take my ice cream while I <u>was eat</u> it.
2. When I <u>was waking</u> up, it was raining hard.
3. I stopped and <u>watch</u> the cats while they were playing.
4. We were waiting at the airport <u>while</u> you called.
5. It was 6 a.m. and people <u>was starting</u> to wake up.
6. I made my partner's breakfast while she <u>getting</u> dressed.
7. We were watching TV when suddenly everything <u>was going</u> dark.
8. I <u>still slept</u> at 8 a.m. this morning when my sister arrived.

5 Complete the article with *the* or no article (–).

Pet choices

Tortoises can make great pets, because they're quiet and don't need a lot of care. They don't need to go out for a walk in ¹............ mornings and in ²............ evenings and you don't need to feed them very often. Just give them ³............ plants that they can eat when they want. Tortoises, like ⁴............ other pets, help you to feel better when you're stressed. But there are some important things to think about. First, think about ⁵............ type of tortoise you want to have. Red-footed tortoises from ⁶............ South America are very popular and make good pets, and so do Indian Star tortoises.

Then, you need to think about the tortoise's home. Tortoises need fresh air and ⁷............ sunlight. They need ⁸............ water, plants and interesting things to look at and touch, like rocks. Also, ⁹............ tortoises like to make holes in ¹⁰............ ground and try to go under things. All of this means that they should be outside as much as possible.

6 Choose the correct word or phrase to complete the sentences.
1. There are twenty chairs in the classroom, but .... them are broken, so not everyone can sit down.
   a none of   **b** some of   **c** lots
2. I've got two children and .... sing well.
   a both of them   **b** all of them   **c** none of them
3. I spend .... of my time at home, but not all.
   a most   **b** none   **c** both
4. You .... to listen to me!
   a all need   **b** all of you need   **c** need all
5. The roads are busy today, but .... cars are moving.
   a all of   **b** some the   **c** most
6. I've got four nephews and .... are really tall!
   a some them   **b** all of them   **c** none of they

16

REVIEW 1–2

VOCABULARY

7 Complete the phrases with a verb. The first letter is given.

1 w................ up at 7 a.m.
2 s................ the window when it's cold
3 b................ your teeth before you go to bed
4 p................ your clothes into a suitcase
5 s................ the light on when it's dark
6 p................ something away in a cupboard
7 l................ the door with a key
8 d................ your hair after you wash it
9 j................ a gym or sports club
10 m................ your family when you're away from home

8 Choose the correct words to complete the blog.

Some people have a ¹**career / work** where they do the same kind of thing their whole lives. Not me! I've had a lot of different jobs. First, I was a ²**cleaner / factory worker**. I put things into boxes at a food company. While I was on holiday with some friends, I got talking to the manager of our hotel and he ³**developed / offered** me a job as a tour guide. It was my ⁴**job / work** to show English-speaking tourists around the area. After a few years, I came home and became a ⁵**dentist / PA** to the manager of a big company. The ⁶**interview / pay** was really good so I had quite a lot of money, but the hours were terrible. I left to ⁷**develop / sign** my own business. I'm the ⁸**author / dancer** of a baking blog, because baking has been my hobby for years. But it's not easy to make money from a blog so now I want to study more about business. In fact, a university ⁹**developed / offered** me a place on a course last week!

9 Match the descriptions (1–6) with the feelings (a–f).

1 want to know more
2 not pleased
3 worried; can't relax
4 sure about something
5 scared and not safe
6 sad because you're alone

a stressed
b afraid
c lonely
d unhappy
e interested
f confident

10 Complete the groups with the animals in the box.

| bear   bird   butterfly   chicken   crocodile |
| fly   rabbit   rat   whale   wolf |

1 small animals with a tail: ...., ...
2 larger animals with fur: ...., ...
3 insects with wings: ...., ...
4 animals with feathers: ...., ...
5 animals that live in water: ...., ...

11 Choose the correct words to complete the sentences.

1 My plane's going to be late. There's a 45-minute **delay / flight**.
2 There were no direct flights from London to San Antonio so we **changed / flew out** in Houston.
3 When we went through **passport control / security**, we had to take off our coats and shoes.
4 We printed our **boarding passes / customs** before we got to the airport.
5 Our flight **boarded / landed** a short time ago. We're in the arrivals hall now.
6 Let's go to the **check-in desk / departure lounge** and get something to eat.
7 Our suitcases should be in **baggage reclaim / passport control** by now.
8 Her plane's **due to arrive / flew out** in about twenty minutes.

12 Complete the email with the words in the box.

| answer (x2)   bring   cancel |
| carry   make (x2)   take (x2) |

Ryan,

I need to travel to our Leeds office later. I'm in meetings all this morning. Could you do these things for me? Thank you!

- ¹................ all of my meetings this afternoon.
- Buy a train ticket and ²................ a reservation for a hotel room in Leeds for tonight.
- ³................ an appointment with Anna at our Leeds office for tomorrow at 9 a.m.
- Book a taxi for 12 p.m. and get someone to ⁴................ my suitcase down at that time.
- ⁵................ a look at my emails and ⁶................ any you can.
- ⁷................ any calls that come through to my desk.
- ⁸................ me a coffee just before my meeting at 11 a.m. I'll need it!
- Get a coffee for yourself and make sure you ⁹................ a break!

Lesson 3A

GRAMMAR | have to, don't have to, can't
VOCABULARY | knowing, understanding and thinking; school and university subjects
PRONUNCIATION | connected speech: have to

VOCABULARY

knowing, understanding and thinking

1 A Choose the correct word or phrase to complete the sentences.

1 I need someone to .... the situation to me.
  a decide   b explain   c develop
2 I've .... that I work best in the mornings.
  a expected   b planned   c discovered
3 We .... a different teacher to the one we have.
  a planned   b searched   c expected
4 We need to .... our work better from now on.
  a develop   b plan   c decide
5 What information should I .... for on the internet?
  a search   b describe   c decide
6 We've .... a system that works very well.
  a decided   b developed   c explained

B Complete the forum post with the words in the box.

decide   describe   develop   discover
expect   explained   plan   search for

@Dani
One hour ago

A teacher once [1]................. to me why it's important to understand how you learn. It's so that you can [2]................. your studies better and you don't waste time on things that don't work for you. The best thing is to try different ways of learning. Ask your friends and other people on your course to [3]................. their study habits and [4]................. some ideas online. Then, try them all out yourself. [5]................. on which ones to use and which ones to forget. For example, try working in the mornings and in the evenings. Take regular breaks and do a bit of exercise. You can [6]................. some interesting things about yourself and [7]................. a learning system that works for you. Don't [8]................. things to change overnight, though. It takes time to really understand yourself.

school and university subjects

2 Complete the descriptions with a school or university subject. The first letter is given.

1 I love knowing how machines work. I'm studying e.................
2 I want to be a teacher. I'm studying e.................
3 I'm really interested in computers. I'm studying i................. t.................
4 I like learning about forests, seas and rivers. I'm studying g.................
5 I want to manage my own company. I'm studying b................. s.................
6 I'm interested in how people manage our country. I'm studying p.................
7 I want to be doctor. I'm studying m.................
8 I'd like to work for a travel company. I'm studying t.................

GRAMMAR

have to, don't have to, can't

3 A The sentences below have a mistake. Choose the best option to correct the mistake.

1 We <u>has to</u> leave now or we'll be late.
  a don't have to   b can't   c have to
2 You <u>don't have to</u> eat here, only in the dining hall.
  a can't   b has to   c haven't
3 I <u>haven't</u> to finish this project until next week.
  a have   b don't have   c can't
4 You <u>can to</u> drive without wearing a seatbelt.
  a can't   b has to   c doesn't have to

B Complete the second sentence so that it means the same as the first. Use have to, don't have to or can't.

1 It's necessary to learn all these words by Friday.
  I .... all these words by Friday.
2 It's not OK to copy work from the internet.
  You .... from the internet.
3 It isn't necessary for my friend to help me, but he likes it.
  My friend ...., but he likes it.
4 It's not OK for children under thirteen to use this website.
  Children under thirteen .... this website.
5 It isn't necessary for you to read this book, but you'll enjoy it.
  You ...., but you'll enjoy it.
6 Is it necessary for us to do this exercise?
  .... this exercise?
7 It's not OK for them to sit here.
  They ....
8 Is it necessary for me to finish the work by tomorrow?
  .... the work by tomorrow?

PRONUNCIATION

4 🔊 **3.01 | connected speech: *have to* |** Listen and complete the sentences with the words you hear.
1 I _____ my manager later.
2 We _____ our work by 5 p.m.
3 Do I _____ to today's meeting?
4 My friends _____ work a lot.
5 Do you _____ in an office?
6 You _____ and see this.

READING

5 Read the text. Choose the correct word to complete the sentence.

Get a book without spending a penny

On the 1st of every month, our readers can enjoy one new e-book for _____. Just click here.

1 zero 2 none 3 free

6A Read the email. Decide which book (1–4) best matches each reader (a–d).
a Leah enjoys reading stories where people change their lives for the better.
b Frank likes books with exciting stories and lots of action.
c René loves stories about families and their lives.
d Seth reads stories about the lives of teenagers.

B Read the email again. Choose the correct option (a or b) to complete the sentences.
1 Alyssa has a problem because she
   a picked up the wrong thing.
   b has lost a lot of money.
2 Theo has to choose between
   a helping his parents and helping his friends.
   b moving away from the farm or staying at the farm.
3 Maribel decides to make a big change because
   a she needs to find a job.
   b she has no friends or partner.
4 At his party, Levi Stone
   a finds out more about his family.
   b meets people he never met before.

C Complete the sentences with one or two words from the text in each gap.
1 Alyssa is staying in a _____ but that's now not safe. She thinks she can get help from someone she met at a _____.
2 Theo feels _____ so he's excited when he sees lights in the _____ and he finds a message.
3 Maribel starts _____ a lot more after she moves to a little _____.
4 Levi Stone and his family must stay together because of a _____. Everyone finds out each other's _____.

From: Online Book World

It's the 1st of the month and time for this month's e-book offer. Choose one of the four amazing books below and get it free.

1 *The money bag*
All Alyssa wanted was a holiday where she could relax and forget about her boring job. But after one mistake at the airport, she now has a suitcase full of money that isn't hers and several people are watching her. A message in her hotel room tells her not to take the money to the police. Now her room isn't safe and she needs to run and hide. Can the man she met at a restaurant help her? Can she get the money back to the owner and stay alive?

2 *Searching for the light*
Life for 17-year-old Theo isn't easy. He lives on a farm in the middle of nowhere. His parents only want him there because he works hard. His school friends only want to know him because he helps them with their homework. He's lonely. When he sees an unusual light in the sky one morning, he follows it into the forest. There, he finds a message. He replies. The lights appear in the sky several more times and so do the messages. Theo has to decide whether to continue his plan to leave the farm or stay and find out about the strange lights.

3 *Starting again*
Maribel decides it's time do something about her life. Alone, in a job she doesn't enjoy and living in an expensive city flat, she decides to move away to a house in a small village by the sea, where she doesn't know anyone. It's the perfect place for starting again and spending more time with her favourite hobby of painting. She soon realises that she made a great decision.

4 *Discovering the past*
It's Levi Stone's 30th birthday party and the Stone family are all together for the first time in ten years – his parents, his brothers and sisters and his cousins. When a snow storm comes, the family has to stay in the same house for a week. The family can no longer hide from each other's questions. Each person has secrets that no one else knows about – secrets that will change their lives forever.

Lesson 3B

GRAMMAR | subject and object questions
VOCABULARY | positive adjectives
PRONUNCIATION | word stress in adjectives

VOCABULARY

positive adjectives

1 A Choose the correct word or phrase to complete the sentences.

1. Watching this show was a really .... idea.
   a favourite   b brilliant   c equal
2. This food tastes absolutely ....!
   a real   b popular   c delicious
3. The author is very .... and makes you think.
   a equal   b clever   c favourite
4. My .... programme is an online science show.
   a favourite   b exciting   c real
5. It's .... to watch women's football on TV.
   a exciting   b favourite   c equal
6. It's a TV show, but it's about .... person.
   a a real   b an equal   c a favourite

B Complete the conversation with the words in the box.

> brilliant   clever   equal   exciting
> favourite   popular   real

A: I'm watching *Stranger Things* at the moment. It's already my ¹............... show!
B: I've heard it's really ²............... around the world. What's it about?
A: A group of school friends in the 1980s.
B: Is it about ³............... life?
A: Not really. One of the friends, Will, goes missing. No one can find him, because he's in a different world, but he learns to use lights to communicate with his mum. Then, the friends meet a strange girl with a ⁴............... skill – she can move things just by thinking of them. The friends need this girl because they're going to fight the bad guys and none of them are particularly big or strong. With the girl and her skills, they can have a more ⁵............... fight.
B: It sounds very ⁶...............!
A: It is, and scary. It's funny, too. There's a character called Steve. He's silly and not very ⁷..............., but he makes me laugh.
B: I should watch it!

PRONUNCIATION

2 🔊 **3.02** | **word stress in adjectives** | Listen and complete the table with the words in the box.

> brilliant   clever   delicious   equal
> exciting   favourite   popular   real

●	●●	●●●	●●●●

GRAMMAR

subject and object questions

3 Choose the correct word or phrase to complete the sentences.

1. What English dictionary ....?
   a use you   b you do use   c do you use
2. Who .... this empty bottle of water here?
   a left   b did they leave   c did left
3. What .... on TV most nights?
   a they watch   b do they watch   c watches
4. What .... to do tonight?
   a do you want   b want you   c did you want
5. Which team .... the match last night?
   a did win   b did they win   c won
6. Which TV channel .... the best TV programmes?
   a did they make   b makes   c do they make

4 Use the prompts in brackets to complete the questions.

¹...............
(What / you / do / last night?)

> I watched a film. I can't remember the name, but it was about a virtual reality world.

Hmm. ²...............
(Who / play / the main part?)

> No idea, but it was a young guy in his twenties, maybe.

³...............
(Who / direct / it?)

> I think it was Steven Spielberg.

Oh! Is it new? ⁴...............
(When / it / come out?)

> In 2018, I think.

(Oh, I know – *Ready Player One*)

⁵...............
(Where / you / watch it?)

> At home on my laptop.

⁶...............
(Who / pay / for your laptop?)
I thought you had no money.

> I got paid yesterday.

⁷...............
(What / you / think of the film?)

> ★★★★

LISTENING

5 🔊 3.03 | Listen to a discussion between two friends. Choose the topic (a–c).

a Best films and TV programmes this year
b What we can learn from films and TV
c Films that came from books

6A 🔊 3.03 | Listen again. Who did these things, the man (M) or the woman (W)?

1 watched a programme about England in the past
2 watched a film about women at NASA
3 learnt what to do when there's a problem in the kitchen
4 learnt that it's important to work with other people
5 cried at the end of a film

B 🔊 3.03 | Listen again. Are the statements True (T) or False (F)?

1 The king in *The Last Kingdom* was a real person.
2 The man thinks that films about the past aren't always correct.
3 The man believes films teach us more about the past than now.
4 The woman says films are important for children.
5 The man talks about how a film ends.

C 🔊 3.04 | Listen to the recording. Write what you hear. You will hear the sentences only once.

1 ....
2 ....
3 ....
4 ....

WRITING

correct mistakes

7A Read the description. Which photo is it about, A or B?

> The photo show an actor in a film studio. he's wearing a dark suit and a white shirt. There are lights with umbrellas next of him. On front of him, there's a television camera and a man. The man is moveing the camera. On the left, there's a man and a woman. They're look at the actor. Behind them, there are some clothes.

B Find and correct six mistakes in the description in Ex 7A.
- two grammar mistakes
- two preposition mistakes
- two spelling or punctuation mistakes

8A Look at photo B. Make notes about these things.
- the place
- the people
- the actions

B You have 9 minutes to write about Photo B. You must write 50–75 words.

C Read your description. Look for any grammar, vocabulary, spelling or punctuation errors and correct them. Look for common mistakes you often make.

Lesson 3C

HOW TO ... | give instructions and check understanding
VOCABULARY | location, position and movement
PRONUNCIATION | intonation in short questions

VOCABULARY

location, position and movement

1 A Choose the correct prepositions to complete the sentences.
1 Shall we put this photo **inside** / **on** the wall so people can see it?
2 It's hot, so I've put your chocolate **out of** / **in** the fridge.
3 There are some huge rain clouds right **above** / **forwards** our house.
4 I'm very silly. I left my bike **into** / **outside** the shop and walked home!
5 How do I get **out of** / **together** this building?
6 To cross the river, go **out of** / **over** the foot bridge.
7 I keep all of my books **inside** / **inside-out** my bedroom cupboard.
8 Shall we go for a walk **around** / **onto** the shops tomorrow?
9 It's starting to rain – let's go **inside-out** / **into** that shop until it finishes.
10 I moved the chair **beside** / **forwards** so I could see the TV better.

B Choose the correct word or phrase to complete the sentences.
1 Let's all stand .... so we don't lose anyone!
  a together   b beside   c towards
2 Why is the coffee table in the living room ....?
  a inside-out   b up and down   c upside-down
3 Walk .... the coffee shop and you'll see me!
  a up and down   b forwards   c towards
4 Please don't jump .... on the bed!
  a altogether   b up and down   c inside-out
5 We moved .... from the snake very quickly!
  a up and down   b away   c beside
6 We're sitting .... the river eating an ice cream.
  a beside   b forwards   c up and down

How to ...

give instructions and check understanding

2 A 🔊 3.05 | Listen to three conversations. Match the problems (1–3) with the hacks (a–c).
1 The man needs to water his new plants.
2 The woman can't see in the mirror after a shower.
3 The children's toys are dirty.
a Use car wax.
b Use the dishwasher.
c Use a plastic bottle with holes in it.

B 🔊 3.05 | Choose the correct words to complete the extracts. Then listen again and check.
1 **First** / **Next**, put some water into the bottle.
2 **First** / **After that**, put the top on the bottle.
3 Is this **like** / **right**?
4 I **meant** / **understood** a small hole, like this.
5 What's wax? I don't know that **meaning** / **word**.
6 You **have** / **should** to put it on the mirror ...
7 But **don't** / **not** put too much on.
8 What do I **should** / **need** to do after that?
9 **Always put** / **Put always** them in a bag first.
10 Let me get one and put the toys in ... **like** / **seem** this?
11 What **all** / **now**?
12 I'm not **know** / **sure** I understand.

PRONUNCIATION

3 🔊 3.06 | intonation in short questions | Listen to the questions. Does the intonation go up (U) or down (D)?
1 That's all?   4 Like this?
2 Is this right?   5 What now?
3 Sorry?   6 OK, what next?

SPEAKING

4 A 🔊 3.07 | Complete the conversation with the words in the box. Then listen and check.

| after that   first   like this   next |
| this   that   understand |

A: I'm really hot and thirsty, but I forgot to put the drinks in the fridge. They're not cold.
B: Put them in the freezer with the ice. You can put a paper towel around them, too. They'll get colder faster.
A: A paper towel? I'm not sure I ¹................ .
B: I read about it online. ²................, take a paper towel and put some water on it so it's wet.
A: ³................ ?
B: Yes. ⁴................, put it around the drink bottle.
A: All right.
B: Not like ⁵................, like ⁶................ .
A: Oh, right. Done! What ⁷................ ?
B: Put it in with the ice in your freezer and wait.
A: Does it work?
B: I don't know. I've never tried it before!

B 🔊 3.08 | You are B in Ex 4A. Listen and speak after the beep. Record the conversation if you can.

C Listen to your recording and compare it to Ex 4A.

Speak anywhere Go to the interactive speaking practice

Lesson 3D

GRAMMAR | *had to, didn't have to, couldn't*
LISTENING | a discussion about memories

GRAMMAR

had to, didn't have to, couldn't

1 Choose the correct word or phrase to complete the sentences.

1 We **couldn't / had to / didn't have to** drink milk every morning at school and I hated it!
2 I loved playing outside in the rain but we **couldn't / had to / didn't have to** do that at school.
3 You **couldn't / had to / didn't have to** help me but I'm happy you did!
4 Schoolchildren of the past **couldn't / had to / didn't have to** have a computer to do their work.
5 Children **couldn't / had to / didn't have to** talk when the head teacher was in the room.
6 I **couldn't / had to / didn't have to** get up early this morning and I'm really tired now!

2 Use the prompts to write sentences with *have to, had to, didn't have to* and *couldn't*.

1 I / stay late at work / yesterday. It was great!
2 We / use the road / this morning. It was closed.
3 You / take the bus / yesterday? Or was your car fixed?
4 My brother / go to school / today. The heating was broken.
5 We / have our weekly team meeting / today. Our manager was not well.
6 Sandro / answer my messages / today. He lost his phone.
7 Alison / work / last week? Or was she on holiday?
8 I / wear / a shirt and jacket at school. It was a school rule.
9 Why / you / work today? I thought you were sick.
10 We / get / a table at the restaurant. It was really busy.

LISTENING

3 A 🔊 **3.09** | Listen to a radio discussion. Choose the topic they do NOT talk about.

a Children and their memories
b Very old people and their memories
c How to remember things better

B 🔊 **3.09** | Listen again. Choose the correct option (a–c) to answer the questions.

1 How old was the presenter in his first memory?
 a two
 b three
 c four
2 When do we start to forget our early memories?
 a when we're three
 b when we're five
 c when we're seven
3 Why does Dr Pasko think the presenter remembers the activity in his first memory?
 a He was excited about it.
 b It was his first time doing something.
 c His parents talked about it a lot after it happened.
4 Which memory idea does Dr Pasko particularly like?
 a taking photos with our phones
 b writing memories on postcards
 c keeping a memory box

C 🔊 **3.09** | Listen again and complete each sentence with one word.

1 The presenter's first memory is of his first ....
2 In Dr Pasko's first memory, she was having fun with ....
3 Maybe children forget memories because their .... are still developing.
4 Dr Pasko says that the activity in her first memory wasn't very ....
5 Dr Pasko suggests writing memories on pieces of paper and putting them into a ....

Lesson 4A

GRAMMAR | present perfect simple (1)
VOCABULARY | irregular past participles
PRONUNCIATION | irregular past participles

VOCABULARY

irregular past participles

1 A Complete the table with the correct words.

infinitive	past participle
be	been
make	1 ....
2	ridden
drink	3 ....
4	done
have	5 ....
6	left
run	7 ....
write	8 ....

B Complete the sentences with the past participle form of the verbs in brackets.

1 My grandparents have never .... (be) anywhere abroad.
2 I've never .... (see) snow except on TV.
3 No one in my family has ever .... (sleep) outside in a tent.
4 I've never .... (swim) in the sea or in a river.
5 Has Dani ever .... (meet) anyone famous, like a singer or a film star?
6 My team has .... (win) a lot of games in the last few months.
7 I haven't .... (read) this book. Do you think I would like it?
8 Have you ever .... (buy) something really expensive?
9 I've .... (eat) pizza in Naples.
10 Have you .... (drive) far in this car?

PRONUNCIATION

2 🔊 **4.01** | **irregular past participles** | Match the past participles (1–6) with a past participle with the same vowel sound (a–f). Then listen and check.

1 ate   a bought
2 been   b drunk
3 caught   c eaten
4 done   d made
5 driven   e met
6 read   f written

1 <u>ate</u> – d m<u>a</u>de

GRAMMAR

present perfect simple (1)

3 A Choose the correct word or phrase to complete the sentences.

1 I've never .... a birthday party.
  a have   b has   c had
2 Have you .... to Thailand?
  a ever been   b never go   c haven't gone
3 We .... a great film last night.
  a see   b saw   c have seen
4 Amara .... in three different countries.
  a live   b has lived   c have lived
5 Zach .... me a lovely present yesterday.
  a gave   b has given   c have given
6 .... you made this meal before?
  a has   b Had   c Have

B Choose the correct verb forms to complete the social media post.

I'm going to be fifty in November. Fifty! There are a lot of things that I ¹**'ve never done / never did** in my life. I ²**'ve never been / never went** camping. I ³**'ve never seen / never saw** a football match except on TV. I ⁴**didn't dance / haven't danced** the tango, and many more things! So, last year I ⁵**'ve written / wrote** a list of fifty things I want to do before I'm fifty. I've done about twenty-seven of them so far. I ⁶**made / 've made** a cake. I ⁷**'ve made / made** it for my friend's birthday in March. I ⁸**'ve ridden / rode** a horse. I ⁹**rode / 've ridden** my friend's horse at the start of May. And I ¹⁰**'ve eaten / ate** sushi. My friends ¹¹**have bought / bought** me some last week. I ¹²**'ve liked / liked** it! I'm excited about doing all of the other things later this year.

C Use the prompts in brackets to complete the conversations.

A: Where's Ryan?
B: (He / go / on a boat trip) ¹.................. . He wants to catch some fish.
A: Oh! (you / ever / go on a fishing trip) ²..................?
B: (No, / I / not) ³.................. . Have you?
A: Yes. (I / go / on one last year) ⁴.................. . We didn't go on a boat. We went to a river. It was a nice day, but (I / not / catch / any fish) ⁵.................. .

A: Maddie wants to go camping. (I / never / do / it / before) ⁶.................. . Have you?
B: Yes, when I was a child, (I / go camping / a lot) ⁷.................. .
A: (I / never / sleep / outside) ⁸.................. . Is it good?
B: It depends on the weather!

LISTENING

4 A 🔊 **4.02** | Listen to a conversation between friends. Choose the activities that each person has done.

	Brett	Carmen
been on a radio show	✓	
won a competition		
won money		
been to Northern Ireland		
been on television		

B 🔊 **4.02** | Listen again. Choose the correct words to complete the sentences.
1 Brett **told / didn't tell** his family about the competition.
2 Brett was **first / second** in the competition.
3 Brett is going to buy a new camera later in the **month / year**.
4 Carmen won a **sport / writing** competition.
5 Brett took the photo in Northern **Ireland / Italy**.
6 Carmen was on a **news / comedy** programme.
7 Carmen **remembers / doesn't remember** the questions she answered.
8 **Carmen / Carmen's friend** was unhappy with the news programme.

C 🔊 **4.02** | Listen again. Complete the summary with one word or number in each gap.

Brett was on the radio because he came second in a ¹_____ competition. He won ²£_____. He took the photo when he was on a ³_____ trip. Carmen was on TV after someone asked her and her friend some questions when they were leaving a ⁴_____. The questions were about a ⁵_____ they saw. Later, Carmen was on TV talking about her experience. She remembers her ⁶_____ looked very big.

D 📝 🔊 **4.03** | Listen to the recording. Write what you hear. You will hear the sentences only once.
1 ....
2 ....
3 ....
4 ....

WRITING

a description of a first-time experience; link ideas

5 A Read the description and answer the questions with a word or number.
1 How many kilometres did the writer run?
2 How many minutes did it take the writer to finish?
3 Does the writer want to run again?

First and last experience

Last autumn, I did something for the first and last time. I ran five kilometres. ¹_____ I walk a lot, I don't often run. When a friend asked me to run five kilometres with her, I said yes. I can walk five kilometres very easily, ²_____ I didn't expect any problems with running. I was wrong. I started running very well. I felt comfortable at first, ³_____ after two kilometres, I started to feel very tired. My friend continued to run well ⁴_____ she's a good runner. It took her about thirty minutes. I walked, then ran, then walked. It took me fifty-five minutes to finish. I love walking, ⁵_____ I never want to run again!

B Complete the description in Ex 5A with the words in the box.

although   because   but (x2)   so

6 A You are going to write a description of the first time you experienced one of the things in the box. Decide what to write about.

a game   a hobby   a new food   a sport
a trip/visit to a new place   an unusual experience

B Make notes on these things:
- what you did
- when you did it
- where you did it
- who you did it with
- why you want (or don't want) to do it again

C Write your description. Link your sentences with the words in Ex 5B where possible. Write 80–120 words.

Lesson 4B

GRAMMAR | comparatives and superlatives
VOCABULARY | travel; travel phrases
PRONUNCIATION | sentence stress

VOCABULARY

travel

1 A Choose the correct word or phrase to complete the sentences.

1 What's the quickest _____ to Manchester from here?
   a direction   **b** route   **c** travel
2 Air _____ is the safest way to travel.
   a trips   **b** travel   **c** way
3 The _____ between Canada and the USA is nearly 9,000 km long.
   a border   **b** direction   **c** distance
4 Let's take a day _____ to somewhere nice!
   a travel   **b** journey   **c** trip
5 Is there a faster _____ to get to the centre of the city?
   a journey   **b** direction   **c** way
6 The _____ from Frankfurt to Sydney took a very long time.
   a direction   **b** journey   **c** travel

B Complete the article with the words in the box.

> borders   direction   distance
> journey   travel   tours   way

Is this the world's most travelled person?

Babis Bizas was born in Greece in 1954. While he was studying languages at university, he travelled around Europe, and then decided to go to Asia where he crossed the ¹_____ of several countries including Afghanistan, Pakistan and India. While he was making his ²_____ through Colombo, Sri Lanka, he decided to take a job on a Greek boat because he needed money. The boat travelled a great ³_____ across the ocean, first in the ⁴_____ of Africa and then on to North America. Babis decided that he wanted to spend his life working in the ⁵_____ industry, so he became a tour guide. Today, Babis takes people on ⁶_____ in places that tourists don't usually visit. He has visited every country in the world, many of them twice or more. He's even been to both the North Pole and the South Pole. His helicopter ⁷_____ to the South Pole took nineteen hours.

travel phrases

2 Use the prompts to make sentences about the places.

1 Sweden is / border / Norway and Finland.
 _____
2 China / other side / world / to Brazil.
 _____
3 California / west coast / the US.
 _____
4 Oman / the other side / Arabian Sea / India.
 _____
5 Istanbul / west / Turkey.
 _____
6 Paris isn't / the coast.
 _____
7 Ethiopia / east coast / Africa.
 _____
8 You can stop / Nicaragua / your way / Mexico / from Ecuador.
 _____

GRAMMAR

comparatives and superlatives

3 A The sentences below have a mistake. Choose the best option to correct the mistake.

1 It's <u>more hot</u> than it was yesterday.
   a hoter   **b** hotter   **c** more hot
2 Who's <u>the funny</u> person in your family?
   a a funnyer   **b** the most funny   **c** the funniest
3 This way isn't <u>the same than</u> the other way.
   a the same as   **b** as same as   **c** as same than
4 Where is the best place <u>to eating</u> around here?
   a eating   **b** eat   **c** to eat

B Complete the conversation with the comparative or superlative form of the adjective in brackets.

A: What do you think is ¹_____ (good) way to travel around a country?
B: For me, it's by motorbike. It's ²_____ (easy) way to get around, but I also enjoy train travel.
A: I imagine that travelling by motorbike is ³_____ (cheap) than travelling by train.
B: It depends on the country. Sometimes, it's ⁴_____ (expensive).
A: I like taking the train. For me, it's ⁵_____ (safe) way to travel and it's a bit ⁶_____ (comfortable). You can just sit back and enjoy the view.
B: You're right. Trains are ⁷_____ (safe) than motorbikes. And they're usually ⁸_____ (quick).
A: But you still prefer motorbikes to trains?
B: Not just trains. I prefer motorbikes to everything! Motorbikes are the ⁹_____ (interesting) way to travel.

26

PRONUNCIATION

4 🔊 **4.04 | sentence stress |** Use the prompts to make questions. Mark the stressed words. Then listen and check.

1 Which / better, / the beach / the mountains?
....
2 Where / popular / travel destination?
....
3 Who / funny, / your sister / your brother?
....
4 What / cheap / way / travel?
....

READING

5 A Read the tour information and answer each question with one word.
1 Which country is the tour in?
2 How many days is the tour?
3 Where does the tour start and end?

B Read the article again. Are the statements True (T) or False (F)?
1 You see the same things in summer and winter.
2 The price is cheaper than usual at the moment.
3 Some food is included in the price.
4 For £1,500, you get a flight to Iceland.
5 There will be no more than eleven people and you on the tour.
6 Someone from the company comes with you on the tour.
7 You pay extra to use the internet on the bus.
8 You need to take different types of clothes.

C On which day (1–7) can you do these things?
a visit the largest town in the north of Iceland
b take photographs of animals that live in the area.
c visit a place with an interesting past
d visit a place by the sea with unusual sand
e visit a place where people play music
f see a place where people have a bath in natural hot water

The Best of Iceland Tour

Spend seven days on this beautiful island, travelling from west to north to east to south. See amazing nature, look for the Northern Lights in the sky in winter and enjoy the midnight sun in summer.

Price: £1,500 (was £1,850)

This includes:
- transport to all destinations.
- hotel accommodation for seven nights, with breakfast.
- whale-watching boat tour.

This does **not** include your flights to and from Iceland or transport to and from the airport.

Why choose our tour?
- Small groups. No more than twelve people per group.
- Great tour guides.
- Comfortable bus with free wifi.

What do you need to bring?
- Clothes for both warm and cold weather. The weather changes fast.

Day 1 - Reykjavik
You arrive in Reykjavik and explore this exciting city. Visit the interesting concert hall and the amazing street art. Try delicious seafood from the island's coast.

Day 2 - Reykjavik to Borgarnes
Your day starts with an early breakfast at your hotel before the tour starts. On your way to the hotel in Borgarnes, you visit the important village of Reykholt in the west. It's tiny, but it has some interesting history.

Day 3 - Borgarnes to Akureyri
Akureyri is a fishing town and the biggest town in the north of Iceland. On the way there, you pass pretty fishing villages and join a three-hour boat trip in Dalvik where you can see whales and dolphins.

Day 4 - Akureyri to Borgarfjörður
Borgarfjörður is a small village on the east coast of the island. On the way there, you visit the beautiful Mývatn lake where you can pay to visit the baths, with their natural hot water from the ground.

Day 5 - Borgarfjörður to Höfn
Visit the east of the island. You pass farms and lakes where you can see local wildlife and finish the day with a three-hour guided walk.

Day 6 - Höfn to Vik
Vatnajökull National Park is where you go today. The main destination is Skaftafell, with its mountains and ice, but on the way, you visit Diamond Beach with its black sand. Your hotel is in Vik.

Day 7 - Vik to Reykjavik
On the way back to Reykjavik, you visit Þingvellir National Park and enjoy the Gullfoss waterfall. You have the evening to enjoy Reykjavik before returning home the next day.

Lesson 4C

HOW TO | make suggestions and recommendations
VOCABULARY | giving gifts
PRONUNCIATION | intonation to show interest

VOCABULARY

giving gifts

1 A Choose the correct word to complete the sentences.

1 I .... a gift from my nephew yesterday.
   a got   **b** took   **c** received
2 I prefer .... gifts to normal ones!
   a unusual   **b** usual   **c** low
3 Let's .... Imran a gift to say 'thank you'.
   a have   **b** receive   **c** get
4 A trip to Paris is a very .... gift.
   a special   **b** low   **c** best
5 This shop has lovely presents at a really .... price.
   a unusual   **b** small   **c** low
6 Have you .... a gift from my sister?
   a taken   **b** received   **c** given

B Match the sentence beginnings (1–6) with the endings (a–f).

1 I need to buy Lois a birthday
2 A gift experience is an unusual
3 She's received
4 I don't like paying a low
5 We're getting our son
6 I need to buy something

a a lovely gift from her neighbours.
b present this weekend.
c special for my dad's birthday.
d thing to give someone.
e a car for his 21st birthday.
f price for a gift for someone special.

How to ...

make suggestions and recommendations

2 A 🔊 4.05 | Listen to the conversation. Choose the presents the friends suggest.

> a book   a clock   a cooking lesson
> mugs   towels   a video game

B 🔊 4.05 | Listen again and complete the sentences with one or two words.

1 Sam's moving into a new home ....
2 People don't usually buy .... for a new home.
3 The man thinks that a .... is a boring gift.
4 Sam already has some ....
5 Sam would like to know how to ....
6 The woman looks at the website of a ....

C 🔊 4.06 | Find and correct one mistake in each sentence. Then listen and check.

1 What can we getting him?
2 So, what we shall get?
3 That's fine of me, but it's not a very exciting idea.
4 Where we should look for one?
5 Why don't we going there later?
6 Do you think he would liking that?
7 Sound good to me.
8 We should to speak to Paola.

PRONUNCIATION

3 🔊 4.07 | intonation to show interest | Listen and decide if the speakers sound interested (I) or not interested (N).

1 That's fine with me.
2 That sounds really exciting.
3 That's an interesting idea.
4 Great idea!
5 Sounds good to me.

SPEAKING

4 A Complete the conversation with the words in the box.

> a bit   could   don't   fine   getting
> go   idea   sounds   sure

A: What shall we buy Kate as a thank you gift?
B: We ¹............... get her some flowers.
A: I'm not ²............... that's a good idea. She's going away in a few days. She won't enjoy them.
B: Oh, right. How about ³............... her a book?
A: That's ⁴............... with me. Or we could get some of that perfume she likes.
B: It's ⁵............... expensive.
A: Yes, you're right. Why ⁶............... we buy her a box of chocolates? She loves chocolates!
B: ⁷............... good to me! I'm happy to go and get some.
A: OK, thanks. You should ⁸............... to that nice shop in the centre of town. They have great chocolate there.
B: Great ⁹...............!

B 🔊 4.08 | Listen and check.

C 🔊 4.09 | You are B in Ex 4A. Listen and speak after the beep. Record the conversation if you can.

D Listen to your recording and compare it to Ex 4B.

Speak anywhere   Go to the interactive speaking practice

Lesson 4D

GRAMMAR | verbs of sensation + adjective or *like*
READING | food from home

GRAMMAR

verbs of sensation + adjective or *like*

1 **Choose the correct word or phrase to complete the sentences.**

1 It .... cold outside so I'm taking my coat.
  a tastes **b** looks **c** smells
2 I put sugar in my tea so it .... nice.
  a smells **b** feels **c** tastes
3 I can .... something strange in the air.
  a sound **b** look **c** smell
4 What does an ugli fruit .... ?
  a look **b** look like **c** look of
5 That strange noise your car is making .... bad.
  a sounds **b** smells **c** feels
6 What is your new phone .... ?
  a look **b** look like **c** like

2 **Use the prompts in brackets to complete the conversation.**

A: What are you eating?
B: It's a dragon fruit.
A: Really? I've never seen one before. (What / it / smell / like?) ¹ .... ?
B: Here, have a smell.
A: Hmm. (It / smell / fresh.) ² .... (It / look / nice, too.) ³ ....
B: I know. I love it!
A: (What / look / like / inside?) ⁴ .... ?
B: It's white.
A: Really? (What / taste / like?) ⁵ .... ?
B: It's not very sweet, but (it / taste / good.) ⁶ .... Do you want to try it?
A: Hmm. Go on then, I'll give it a try!

READING

3 **Read the blog post. Complete each sentence with one or two words.**

1 The writer is writing about a dish called ....
2 The dish comes from an area in England called ....
3 The dish is potatoes on top of meat, onion and ....

4 **Read the blog post again and choose the correct words to complete the sentences.**

1 In the past, many **bakers / factory workers** cooked Lancashire hotpot at home.
2 They made hotpot because it was **cheap / easy to make**.
3 **Everyone / Not everyone** used their own kitchen to make hotpot.
4 There **are / aren't any** vegetables in Lancashire hotpot.
5 There **is / isn't** only one way to make hotpot.
6 The writer's family ate hotpot on **Mondays / at weekends**.
7 The writer's family life **was / wasn't** always positive.
8 Lancashire hotpot **is / isn't** the writer's children's favourite dish.

The taste of home

There's one dish that always makes me think of home: Lancashire hotpot. Lancashire is an area in the north west of England, close to Manchester. In the 1800s, there were a lot of factories there and many people in the area worked at them. Their work wasn't easy. They worked long days and had little time off. The work was hard and often dirty. When they got home, they were tired and wanted a good meal, but they didn't have the time or energy to make one. So they made hotpot. They could put the food in a pot in the oven in the morning and leave it to cook slowly on a low heat all day. It was ready to eat by the end of the day. Of course, many of those people had no oven in their homes, so they probably took it to the local baker to cook.

Lancashire hotpot is a dish with meat, onions, and carrots and slices of potato on the top. There are other things in it too, like salt, to give it some taste, but those are the main ingredients. It might not sound very tasty to you, but to me it's the most wonderful food in the world. Everyone makes it a bit differently, so there's no single recipe. I think my family's recipe is the best. When I was growing up, my parents often made it for Sunday lunch and my brothers and sisters all loved it. When I taste it now, I think of those Sundays and feel that life was much easier then. But of course, it wasn't without problems. We had some difficult times, but those times when we were together enjoying a hotpot seemed to be some of the best ones. That's why I love making it for my children now. The thing is, they prefer pizza.

3-4 REVIEW

GRAMMAR

1 Read the office rules and complete the sentences. Use *have to*, *don't have to* or *can't* and a verb from the sign.

Office rules

Start work on time at 9 a.m.

Book a meeting room for meetings.

Dress well. Wearing a suit isn't necessary, but no wearing jeans.

No listening to music.

No eating food at your desk.

Be kind to your colleagues.

Introduce yourself to new staff.

It's not necessary to bring cake for everyone on your birthday, but it's nice!

1 We .... work at 9 a.m.
2 We .... a meeting room for meetings.
3 We .... a suit.
4 We .... jeans.
5 We .... to music.
6 We .... food at our desks.
7 We .... kind to our colleagues.
8 We .... ourselves to new staff.
9 We .... cake on our birthday.

2 Look at the answers and complete the questions.

1 Q: Where .... when you were a child?
   A: I lived in a town called Hilden.
2 Q: Who .... to the train station this morning?
   A: My wife took me.
3 Q: Who .... dinner at your house?
   A: My husband and I cook together most nights.
4 Q: When .... to this area?
   A: We moved to this area ten years ago.
5 Q: Where .... spend her weekends?
   A: Anna spends her weekends at home.
6 Q: What .... you happy?
   A: My family makes me happy.

3 The sentences below have a mistake. Choose the best option to correct the mistake.

1 We <u>didn't had to</u> study yesterday but we wanted to.
   a couldn't   b hadn't to   c didn't have to
2 We <u>couldn't</u> our phones during the wedding last week.
   a can't use   b couldn't use   c couldn't to use
3 Jasmine <u>have to</u> start work at 7 a.m. this morning.
   a didn't had to   b had to   c couldn't to
4 Why <u>had you</u> to take your car to the garage yesterday?
   a did you have   b hadn't you   c did you had

4 Complete the sentences with the present perfect or past simple form of the verbs in brackets.

1 I .... (go) to Sweden, but not Denmark.
2 He .... (never / have) long hair.
3 We .... (meet) our new neighbour yesterday.
4 Karen .... (meet) some interesting people in her new job so far.
5 .... (you / enjoy) your holiday last month?
6 Maria .... (go) to Berlin in 2021.
7 Where's Jeff? .... (he / go) home?
8 .... (you / ever / see) a film outdoors?

5 Read the social media post. Choose the correct words to complete the sentences.

Martin Coombes
4 hours ago

I'm visiting Ryde soon. I'd like to take my children to the beach, but I know there are a few beaches in the area. Which one is the ¹**best / better**?

Dana Gibbs
1 hour ago

Each one is a bit different ²**as / from** the other, so you could try a different one each day! Bembridge beach is ³**quieter than / the quietest**, but that's because there are rocks but no sand on the beach. Sandown beach has sand. It's ⁴**more popular / the most popular** beach in the area, but it's also ⁵**busier than / the busiest**. It's ⁶**further / the furthest** away than Bembridge, too. Probably the best beach is Appley Beach. It's similar ⁷**from / to** Sandown, but it's a bit ⁸**quieter / quietest**. There are also two good cafés at Appley. One is a little ⁹**more expensive than / the most expensive** the other but they're both great. Whichever beach you go to, you'll have ¹⁰**more fantastic / the most fantastic** time.

6 Complete the sentences with the words in the box.

| feels   feeling   look   looks   sounds |
| smells   taste   tastes |

1 This apple .... delicious! It's so sweet.
2 You .... tired. Did you not sleep well?
3 This jumper .... really soft on my skin.
4 This cake .... lovely. Is there lemon in it? I can't wait to try it.
5 I've seen polenta, but I've never eaten it. What does it .... like?
6 Marta .... like her dad. They've got the same eyes and nose.
7 I love Noel's singing – he always .... amazing.
8 I'm not .... very well today.

30

REVIEW 3–4

VOCABULARY

7 Choose the correct words to complete the phrases.
1 **discover / search** for information on the internet
2 **explain / expect** a problem to someone
3 **discover / plan** a new word in English
4 **decide / develop** a new system at work
5 **explain / plan** a study day
6 **decide / describe** a person
7 **expect / search** something to happen
8 **decide / discover** on what to eat tonight

8 Match the people (1–8) with the subjects they probably studied (a–h).
1 office manager
2 actor
3 doctor
4 museum tour guide
5 bank manager
6 scientist
7 lawyer
8 sports person

a physical education (PE)
b economics
c science
d medicine
e history
f drama
g law
h business studies

9 Choose the correct words to complete the sentences.
1 Please move **away from / over** the fire.
2 I'll wait out **outside / together** while you get ready.
3 Let's try putting the painting on the wall **above / around** the chair.
4 Your T-shirt is **inside-out / together**. You should put it on properly!
5 The brothers are all standing **together / towards** over there.
6 Kate is the woman over there, standing **beside / inside** the blue car.
7 Let's walk all **around / forwards** the park.
8 Our daughter loves to jump **into / onto** the table!

10 Write the past participle of each verb.
1 give
2 swim
3 buy
4 ride
5 see
6 drive
7 catch
8 win
9 teach
10 drink

11 Complete the conversation with one word in each gap. The first letter is given.

A: What are you doing this weekend?
B: I'm going on a weekend ¹t................. to Berwick-upon-Tweed.
A: Oh nice! Where is that?
B: It's on the ²w................. to Edinburgh from here.
A: Is it on the ³b................. of England and Scotland?
B: That's right. It's also on the ⁴c................., so we can walk near the sea.
A: Oh nice! I've been to Carlisle. It's also in the north, but it's on the other ⁵s................. of the country.
B: Oh yes, I know it. Anyway, it's a long car ⁶j................. to Berwick-upon-Tweed from here. We have to leave straight after work.
A: Yes, which ⁷r................. are you going to take?
B: I think we'll take the M1 then A1.
A: Good idea. You could take the A1 the whole way. It's a shorter ⁸d................., but usually has worse traffic, so, the ⁹t................. time is longer.

12 Complete the forum post with the words in the box.

| exciting | favourite | get |
| present | received | special |

I've ¹................. some great gifts over the years, but my ²................. gift didn't cost anything. It was my thirtieth birthday and my friends decided that they wanted to give me something ³.................. So they each took a small piece of paper and wrote me a message. They wrote something they remembered about me from the past. They put thirty of these pieces of paper into a lovely box, along with some old photos. I got this ⁴................. at my birthday dinner. It was ⁵................. to read each message and look at the photos, because they helped me to remember some funny things from my life. So next time you need to ⁶................. someone a gift, think about something that only costs your time. Your friends will love it!

Lesson 5A

GRAMMAR | possessive pronouns, *whose*, *this/that*, *there/then*
VOCABULARY | money and value
PRONUNCIATION | sounds /s/ and /z/

VOCABULARY

money and value

1 A Choose the correct word or phrase to complete the sentences.

1 The price of petrol is .... every day.
   a costing   b spending   c increasing
2 I bought this sofa for a very .... price.
   a fair   b valuable   c expensive
3 Let's .... a car and go to the beach.
   a increase   b rent   c offer
4 I'll use some of my .... to buy a car.
   a savings   b prices   c notes
5 I've had a few .... to buy my car.
   a offers   b money   c savings
6 I didn't spend very much .... my suit.
   a in   b on   c at

B Complete the conversation with the words in the box.

| cost   fair   increase   offer   rent |
| savings   spent   valuable |

A: That's a nice watch. Did it ¹............ much?
B: I think I ²............ about £20 on it.
A: That seems ³............ . It's a lovely watch.
B: Yes, but a friend said it's actually quite ⁴............ .
A: Really? Like thousands of pounds?
B: No. He made me a good ⁵............ of £300.
A: Wow, from £20 to £300. That's amazing! You could ⁶............ a boat for the day. You've always wanted to do that.
B: I know, that would be great, but I said no.
A: Did he ⁷............ his offer?
B: No, he didn't have enough ⁸............ at the time. I told him he can have it when I get bored of it. He'll have enough money then!

GRAMMAR

possessive pronouns, *whose*, *this/that*, *there/then*

2 A The sentences below have a mistake. Choose the best option to correct the mistake.

1 This isn't my bag, it's <u>you</u>.
   a you're   b your   c yours
2 David's not here, but I need to tell <u>he</u> something.
   a his   b him   c he's
3 <u>It's ours</u> cake, not just mine.
   a It's our   b It's my   c Its ours
4 Our train arrives at 6 p.m. so we'll see you <u>when</u>.
   a that   b there   c then

B Complete the sentences with the words in the box. There are three words you do not need.

| her   its   mine   ours   she   that |
| theirs   then   those   whose   who's |

1 Don't worry if you forgot your wallet. I've got .... with me.
2 Do I have to talk to Melanie? I never know what to say to ....
3 An old friend gave me flowers last week. I thought .... was kind of her.
4 The dog is waving .... tail. I think it likes you!
5 My apartment is just five minutes from my parent's apartment. Mine is on the street behind ....
6 I'm going to see Max this evening so I'll tell him your happy news ....
7 .... that man over there? Is it Adam?
8 I can't believe you and I live in houses on the same street. .... is over there. Where's yours?

C Complete the article with a pronoun, *then* or *there*.

Each year, people leave many things on London trains and buses: umbrellas, mobile phones, keys, clothes and toys. Staff find ¹............ things and send them to the Transport for London Lost Property Office. About a thousand things arrive ²............ each day. So, what happens to ³............ ? Well, first of all, staff try to find out ⁴............ item it is. Then, they try to call or write to that person, and the owner has two weeks to come and get ⁵............ . However, often the staff don't know who the owner is, so they save information about the thing to a computer file, explaining what it is, when it arrived, ⁶............ colour or size, etc. Sometimes the owner calls to ask for their lost thing back and the staff return it to ⁷............ . Most of the time, owners don't ask for ⁸............ things back, so the staff give them to charity or throw them away. The office has been open for almost a hundred years. In ⁹............ time, the staff have looked after 15 million objects!

PRONUNCIATION

3 🔊 5.01 | sounds /s/ and /z/ | Listen and match the words in the box with the sounds.

| books   is   its   Matt's   ours   scarf |
| this   theirs   whose   yours |

/s/ ...., ..., ..., ..., ...
/z/ ...., ..., ..., ..., ...

5A

READING

4 A Read the article. Match the stories (1–4) with the headings (a–d).
  a Art by a famous painter
  b A diamond that was real
  c A lucky gamer
  d A field of gold

Look what I found!

1 ....

In 2019, Scott Amos was in California, in the US, visiting the house he grew up in. He was looking in some boxes when he found an old video game called Kid Icarus. It was probably a gift to him when he was young, but no one in the family remembered it. The 1987 video game wasn't open and it looked perfect. Scott talked to someone who knew a lot about video games, and found out that there were only ten games in perfect condition in the world. The game originally cost $38.45. Scott sold it for $9,000 and used the money for a family trip.

2 ....

In 2014, the owners of a house in Toulouse, France, found some old clothes in a room at the top of the house. They also found a painting there. They thought the painting might be valuable, so they showed it to someone who knew about art. After five years, the owners learnt that the painting was by the famous Italian artist Caravaggio and it was over 400 years old. Not everyone was sure the painting was by Caravaggio, but it was expected to sell for around $171 million. Someone bought it in 2019, but we don't know who or how much they paid.

3 ....

In 2009, British man Terry Herbert went out with a cheap, old metal detector – a machine for finding metal under the ground – to a farmer's field. After walking just 73 metres, the machine made a noise. Terry made a hole in the ground and he found something gold. He made the hole bigger until, after a few days, he had 244 gold and silver objects. Later, he had more than 4,000 things, all over 1,400 years old. It's the largest number of gold and silver items from that time. Two museums bought them for £3 million. Herbert and the farmer shared the money.

4 ....

In the 1980s, a British woman bought an old ring for £10. She didn't know it had a real diamond on it and many years later, decided to put it in the rubbish. Her neighbour saw it and asked the woman to check if the ring was valuable or not. The woman did and discovered the diamond was real. The ring later sold for a huge £656,750.

B Are the statements True (T) or False (F)?
  1 Scott Amos found something valuable at his home.
  2 Scott sold the game and saved the money in a bank.
  3 It was a long time before the owners of the painting in Toulouse discovered who painted it.
  4 We know what the new owner paid for the painting.
  5 Terry Herbert got £3 million for the things he found.
  6 The British woman found a ring in a rubbish bin.

C Complete the sentences with one word or a number.
  1 Scott thinks the game was a .... for him as a child.
  2 Caravaggio painted the picture over .... years ago.
  3 Terry Herbert found more than .... objects.
  4 The woman's .... told her to check if the ring was valuable.

WRITING

a description of a past event

5 A Read the description. What happened to Larry Awe?
  a He lost something valuable to him.
  b He found something, but it wasn't valuable.
  c He discovered something that might be valuable.

More than an old shoe

Larry Awe was cleaning out an old shopping centre. His job was to throw away anything left [1]............... before builders came to take down the building, but when Larry found some boxes with old basketball shoes inside, he knew he couldn't throw [2]............... away. They were all shoes of famous basketball players. Larry knew [3]............... because the shoes had the players' names on them. One of [4]............... was Michael Jordan's famous Air Jordan shoe. The words 'My Very Best' and [5]............... name were on the shoe. Jordan wore it around 1985, early in [6]............... career as a basketball player. [7]............... makes the shoe very valuable. [8]............... could be worth up to $20,000.

B Complete the description in Ex 5A with *it*, *his*, *this*, *them* or *there* to avoid repeating words.

6 A You are going to write a description of something valuable that a man called Paul Raynard found. Read the notes.
  • Paul Raynard – English. Visiting Ballycastle in Northern Ireland with friend Michael.
  • Went to field to look for Michael's wedding ring – lost there.
  • One hour – nothing. Later one gold coin, two gold coins, three gold coins – eighty-four gold coins!
  • One very valuable – £6,000.
  • All coins now in Ulster Museum. Worth £100,000.
  • Never found wedding ring.

B Plan your description. Decide what information to include and the order of information.

C Write your description. Use pronouns and *there*/*then* so you don't repeat ideas. Write 80–120 words.

Lesson 5B

GRAMMAR | quantifiers
VOCABULARY | countable and uncountable nouns
PRONUNCIATION | weak forms in quantifiers

VOCABULARY

countable and uncountable nouns

1 A Put the words in the box in the correct column.

~~accommodation~~ ~~apartment~~ dollar fashion food hour jumper meal money music song time

countable nouns	uncountable nouns
apartment	accommodation

B Choose the correct word or phrase to complete the sentences.

1 I haven't got much **dollars** / **euros** / **money** on me.
2 She's always very tired after **hour** / **job** / **work** on a Friday.
3 Can I share these photos on **news** / **post** / **social media**?
4 We've found a really great **accommodation** / **apartment** / **fashion** to rent.
5 This is a really lovely **fashion** / **jumper** / **meals**.
6 Have we got enough **dollar** / **hour** / **time** for a coffee?

C Look at the sentence beginnings (1–10). Which sentences do you complete with a and which with b?

1 You've got a lot of
2 I'm only bringing one
   a suitcase for the trip.
   b luggage for a weekend trip.
3 Our living room clock needs a
4 The house has no
   a new battery.
   b electricity at the moment.
5 I've got a great
6 I need some
   a advice on how to cook for ten people.
   b suggestion for our meal out.
7 I read a really interesting
8 I usually read
   a news on social media.
   b article earlier.
9 You can take a few pieces of
10 We've only got a bit of
   a paper from the printer.
   b food in the house.

GRAMMAR

quantifiers

2 A Choose the correct word or phrase to complete the sentences.

1 There .... much food in the fridge.
   a aren't   b isn't   c is no
2 Would you like .... coffee?
   a some   b too much   c many
3 There's .... time for us to chat.
   a many   b any   c no
4 Life is .... quiet in this town.
   a enough   b too   c too much
5 Can I have a piece of ...., please?
   a teas   b cakes   c paper
6 There aren't .... chairs for everyone.
   a too many   b too much   c enough
7 I've only got a .... time before my train comes.
   a bit   b little   c lot
8 We don't have .... fruit at home. Can you buy some at the market?
   a many   b no   c any

B Complete the post with the quantifiers in the box.

a lot   any   no   some (x2)   too much

Carla
35 minutes ago

I've just read an interesting article about slow living. ¹............... of people believe a slow life is better for us because we take time to think about what we're doing and enjoy it more. However, not everyone wants a slow life. ²............... people, like me, enjoy a fast life. It helps us to feel alive. So, which is better, a fast life or a slow life? Life can become boring when there are ³............... exciting activities at all, but ⁴............... excitement can make you tired and stressed. So, we probably need both a fast and a slow life. For example, one weekend, we should do ⁵............... exciting things and the next weekend we shouldn't do ⁶............... exciting activities. By living a fast and slow life, we get the best of both worlds.

5B

PRONUNCIATION

3 🔊 5.02 | **weak forms in quantifiers** | Listen and write the sentences you hear. Then, mark the words in the quantifiers which use a weak /ə/ sound (like the vowel sound in *the*).

1 ....
2 ....
3 ....
4 ....
5 ....

LISTENING

4 🔊 5.03 | Listen to the recording. Choose the words in the text that are different from what you hear.

Slow cities are where people can have a slower life. They can walk or cycle around. There are green spaces for people to visit. The food in restaurants and supermarkets is always local and organic and people enjoy healthy eating. People also care about the culture of the city.

5 A 🔊 5.04 | Listen to an interview about living a slow life. Number the topics (a–e) in the order you hear them.

a   eating
b   a tip for starting a slow life
c   nature
d   work
e   free time

B 🔊 5.04 | Listen again and choose the correct option (a–c) to complete the statements.

1 Jay says it's possible to have a slow life in a fast city by changing
   a the job you do.
   b the way you do things.
   c the flat you live in.
2 Jay changed his working week by
   a working from 8 a.m. to 6 p.m.
   b working only four days a week.
   c working from home.
3 In his free time, Jay began to
   a switch off his phone.
   b stop reading the news.
   c spend more time online than before.
4 Once a week, Jay and his wife
   a invite friends for dinner.
   b talk about their day during dinner.
   c eat dinner without speaking.
5 Jay looks at the trees around him when he
   a walks to the shops.
   b goes running.
   c cycles to work.
6 Jay suggests that the presenter
   a plans to do just a few things each day.
   b wakes up earlier each morning.
   c is nice to people she meets.

C Choose the correct words to complete the sentences.

1 Jay says that apartments in New York are not cheap to **buy** / **rent**.
2 Jay ends work on a **Thursday** / **Friday**.
3 Jay thinks that time on social media is a **good** / **bad** use of time.
4 In the past, Jay ate his dinner in front of **his wife** / **the TV**.
5 Jay thinks that a list of **five** / **twenty** things to do each day is a bad idea.

D 🔊 5.04 | Listen again and check.

6 🔊 5.05 | Listen to the recording. Write what you hear. You will hear the sentences only once.

1 ....
2 ....
3 ....
4 ....

Lesson 5C

HOW TO ... | talk about a product
VOCABULARY | common adjectives
PRONUNCIATION | phrasing

VOCABULARY

common adjectives

1 A Choose the correct word or phrase to complete the sentences.

1 Is the colour of this shirt too .... ?
  a heavy b thin c bright
2 This suitcase is too .... for me to carry.
  a thick b heavy c soft
3 I'd like a winter hat in a .... blue colour.
  a heavy b light c thick
4 This jumper is so .... to touch.
  a bright b soft c light
5 My old socks were thin, but these are lovely and ....
  a thick b light c weak
6 This street is too .... for cars.
  a wide b thin c narrow

B Write the opposite of each adjective.

1 dry .... 5 wide ....
2 empty .... 6 cool ....
3 strong .... 7 heavy ....
4 dark .... 8 thick ....

How to ...

talk about a product

2 A 5.06 | Listen to someone talking about a product. What's the product?
  a a knife b a notebook c a wallet

B 5.06 | Complete the talk with one word in each gap. Then listen and check.

We all want delicious butter with jam in the mornings, but lots of ¹............... find it difficult to put cold, hard butter on our bread. Well, ²............... the answer. It's the Better Butter knife. It's light and comfortable to hold. It's ³............... small holes in it, so it picks up the butter really easily and spreads it across the bread perfectly. But that's not ⁴............... . It can also cut slices of cheese, so it's a butter knife and a cheese knife. Another good ⁵............... about this butter knife is its price. It's just £6.99. I really love my Better Butter knife and you're ⁶............... to love yours, too. It's something that every kitchen should have.

C Choose the correct words to complete the talk.

We all ¹**need** / **see** to look after our things, but what about when we go to the beach for a swim in the sea? It's not always safe ²**enough** / **too** to leave your wallet on the beach when you go into the water. So here's a solution if you're looking for something ³**different** / **usual**! It's the Safe and Dry Wallet. It's not just a ⁴**normal** / **strange** wallet and I'll tell you ⁵**what** / **why**. You ⁶**can** / **do** put it in water and everything inside – cards, cash and even photos – all stay completely dry. ⁷**Think** / **Speak** about it. You can enjoy going to the beach without worrying about your stuff! The wallet costs just £19.99 and it ⁸**comes** / **goes** in six different colours.

PRONUNCIATION

3 5.07 | phrasing | Divide the talk in Ex 2C into phrases. Then listen and check.

We all need to look after our things // but what about when we go to the beach // for a swim in the sea?

SPEAKING

4 A 5.08 | Complete the conversation with the words in the box. Then listen and check.

> another answer best comes
> got know perfect problem

A: Hello. What are you selling today?
B: Hi! Do you have a pet?
A: Yes, I've got a cat.
B: Do you have a ¹............... with pet hair on your clothes?
A: Yes, I do! It's awful!
B: Well, here's the ²............... . Look at this glove. It's ³............... a brush on one side, so you can brush your pet with it and stop fur getting on your clothes.
A: That's interesting.
B: The ⁴............... thing about it is that it's easy to use. You just put it on and brush your pet, then give it a quick clean.
A: That sounds good.
B: ⁵............... good thing about it is that pets love it. And we ⁶............... that it's important to look after our pets.
A: Yes, true. Does it come in just one size?
B: No, it ⁷............... in three different sizes so it's ⁸............... for big, medium and small pets.
A: Great! I'll take a small one.

B 5.09 | You are B in Ex 4A. Listen and speak after the beep. Record the conversation if you can.

C Listen to your recording and compare it to Ex 4A.

Speak anywhere Go to the interactive speaking practice

Lesson 5D

GRAMMAR | verbs with two objects
LISTENING | renting and borrowing

GRAMMAR

verbs with two objects

1 A The sentences below have a mistake. Choose the best option to correct the mistake.

1 Mona is going to <u>show to us her photos</u> later.
   a show her photos us
   b show her photos to us
   c show her photos for us
2 Can you <u>lend your coat for me</u>?
   a lend to me your coat?
   b lend your coat?
   c lend me your coat?
3 I'm going to <u>buy to me a car</u> next week!
   a buy a car
   b me buy a car
   c buy a car to me
4 Jack has <u>left a note you</u>.
   a left a note to you.
   b left for you a note.
   c left you a note.

B Match the sentence beginnings (1–5) with the endings (a–e).

1 I got a
2 We gave
3 Let's get a gift
4 I'm going to get a
5 I gave a gift

a our teacher a thank you gift.
b small gift for Ben and Ela.
c to our neighbour last week.
d lovely gift yesterday.
e for Susi and Megan.

C Put the words in brackets in the correct order to complete the conversations.

Conversation 1

A: ¹............... (spare concert ticket / Simon / my / offered / I / to).
B: ²............... (you / he ask / for / Did / it)?
A: No, but I thought he'd like it, so ³............... (him / I / a message / sent). He hasn't replied. ⁴............... (a call / give / Shall / him / I)?
B: Yes, good idea. Say that ⁵............... (want / to / to give / someone else / the ticket / you). He'll give you an answer then!

Conversation 2

A: I need a laugh. ⁶............... (a joke / me / Tell).
B: I don't know any jokes. No one in my family can ever remember them.
A: That's sad. ⁷............... (everyone in your family / a joke book / buy / I'll / for) when I next visit.

LISTENING

2 A 🔊 5.10 | Listen to two people talking about borrowing something. Answer the questions.

1 What does the man want to borrow?
2 What does his friend suggest using?

B 🔊 5.10 | Listen again. Complete the notes with one word you hear in each gap.

> **How to borrow something you need**
> 1 Rent it from a ....
> 2 Borrow it from your ....
> 3 Ask your .... for one.
> 4 Look for a .... social media group where people give away free things.
> 5 Use an app where you can lend and borrow things, e.g. a .... for a family party, a camera for great photos or an electric .... for your band.

C Choose the correct words to complete the sentences.

1 The man doesn't want to rent from a shop because it's too **expensive / far**.
2 The man can't ask his friends because they **don't have / need** their bikes.
3 The man doesn't want to ask his neighbours because he doesn't **know / like** them.
4 The man doesn't want to take someone's free bike because he doesn't **have space in his flat / live on the ground floor**.
5 The woman thinks the man can get enough money from the app to pay for a **weekend trip / holiday in another country**.

D 🔊 5.10 | Listen and check.

Lesson 6A

GRAMMAR | adverbs of frequency and manner
VOCABULARY | sports collocations (*play, do, go*)
PRONUNCIATION | sentence stress: modifiers with adverbs

VOCABULARY

sports collocations (*play, do, go*)

1 Name the sport or activity for each description.
1 You hit a white ball on a table with a long, thin piece of wood and try to hit balls of other colours.
2 You put on special shoes and move along ice.
3 You run 100 or 800 metres, or do a long jump.
4 You play in a team. You have to hit a ball and then run around a field.
5 You throw a big, heavy ball and try to hit ten other items with it.
6 You play in a team and throw a ball which looks like a large egg.
7 You swim with oxygen under the sea.
8 You play in a team of six. You hit a ball with your hands over a high net.

2 A Choose the correct word or phrase to complete the sentences.
1 Shall we .... bowling tonight?
  a do   **b** go   **c** play
2 I've never .... table tennis before.
  a done   **b** been   **c** played
3 My neighbour .... t'ai chi in the garden most mornings.
  a does   **b** goes   **c** plays
4 I .... hockey for my school's team.
  a did   **b** went   **c** played
5 My wife .... judo, but I've never tried it.
  a does   **b** goes   **c** plays
6 Would you like to .... snowboarding or skiing next winter?
  a do   **b** go   **c** play

B Complete the article with *doing*, *going* or *playing* and a sport in the box.

> bowling cricket exercise karate
> running skiing windsurfing

Sport isn't just about your body. It's about your mind, too. For example, you can:
- feel part of a team and make new friends by ¹.......... or basketball.
- learn about different world cultures by ².........., judo or t'ai chi.
- enjoy nature by ³.......... with an athletics club across fields and through woods.
- experience ocean life by ⁴.......... or sailing.
- see amazing mountain views in winter by ⁵...........
- have fun by ⁶.......... or playing snooker with friends.

So, you see, sport isn't just about ⁷........... It's so much more than that.

GRAMMAR

adverbs of frequency and manner

3 A The sentences below have a mistake. Choose the best option to correct the mistake.
1 <u>Never we go skiing</u> in the winter.
  a We go skiing never
  b We never go skiing
  c We go never skiing
2 <u>Not often Sam is late for</u> our yoga class.
  a Sam isn't late often
  b Sam not often is late
  c Sam isn't often late
3 You played snooker <u>brilliant</u> today.
  a brilliant
  b brilliantly
  c brilliantily
4 Our new football field <u>looks well</u>.
  a looks good
  b well looks
  c good looks

B Put the words in brackets in the correct place in the sentences (1–12). Change the form of the adjectives if necessary.

Comments

John
¹I go cycling at the weekends (normal).
²I enjoy running, but I don't run (very often).
³When I go running, I run (very slow).

Sophie
⁴I'm in the pool at the sports centre (often).
⁵I enjoy it, but I don't swim (brilliant). ⁶I play badminton (bad)!

Jason
⁷I do sport (never). ⁸In the evenings, I fall asleep before 9 p.m. (quite often). I'm too tired for exercise!

Leigh
⁹I ride my bike to work (always). ¹⁰It's fifteen kilometres there and back so I have to cycle (quite hard).

Elizabeth
¹¹In the summer, I go to the sailing club in the mornings (early). ¹²I've got my own boat and I can sail it (quite good).

38

6A

PRONUNCIATION

4 🔊 **6.01 | sentence stress: modifiers with adverbs |** Listen and choose the stressed words in each sentence.

1 I can run quite fast.
2 I don't do it very well.
3 We go there quite often.
4 She does it really brilliantly.
5 We need to move it carefully.

READING

5 📄 Read the text below. Select a picture to answer the question.

> **Team sports**
>
> Do you enjoy team sports? Do you play baseball, cricket or hockey?
> If so, we'd like to hear from you!

Which is the correct picture for the text?

A

B

C

6 A Read the review of an exercise app. Choose the correct word to complete the summary.

The writer thinks people **should / shouldn't** try it.

B Read the review again. Choose the opinions (1–8) that the writer gives.

1 Some free apps are better than this app.
2 It's good that people can try the app for free.
3 The cost of the app is fine.
4 You feel like you're at a real-life exercise class.
5 The app is good for people with busy lives.
6 There are only a few types of exercise class.
7 The information about healthy eating isn't useful.
8 The app is for people who want to exercise hard.

C Read the review again. Are the statements True (T) or False (F)?

1 The app is free for the first month.
2 All the exercises classes are live.
3 The app has lots of different exercise classes.
4 Exercise classes are no longer than an hour.
5 It's hard to find the right exercise classes for you.
6 On your phone, you can do an exercise class from the app or listen to your own music, but not both.

 **REVIEWS**

FITNESS@pp

Health apps are very popular and new ones come out all the time. FITNESS@pp is one of those new apps. Its purpose is to help people do exercise and live a healthy life. So, why should you get the app?

Well, firstly, it's free for fourteen days, so you can try it before you pay the full £15 monthly cost. I think this is important because it stops some people from wasting money. There are cheaper apps, but FITNESS@pp has a lot to offer and the cost seems good to me.

There are live exercises classes every day – fifteen of them. These are great because you can feel part of a real class when you're actually at home. There are also hundreds of video lessons to choose from. It means that busy people like me can exercise at any time of the day.

There are many different types of classes, from ten-minute lessons to sixty-minute ones, from yoga to t'ai chi to using an exercise bike. Some are easy, but many of them are quite hard. This app probably isn't for people who just want easy exercise.

When you start using the app, you answer some questions and the app suggests some exercise classes for you. This helps you to find the right classes easily. The app sends you a message thirty minutes before a live class, so you remember it's happening. It also sends you 'well done' messages after a class, which made me feel good and like I wanted to do more! The app is mostly easy to use.

As well as exercise classes, there is also help with choosing healthy food to eat. The information comes from doctors and other people who understand health well. The advice is good and there are some great meal ideas. I like the fact that the app helps me to stay healthy and also to find food I can enjoy.

The app isn't perfect. I can't play my own music on my phone and use the app at the same time, but there's lots to enjoy. I think anyone interested in exercise should give the fourteen free days a try.

Lesson 6B

GRAMMAR | present perfect simple (2)
VOCABULARY | actions; physical actions
PRONUNCIATION | weak and strong forms: *have, has*

VOCABULARY

actions

1 Match the sentence beginnings (1–6) with the endings (a–f).

1 I think someone's taken
2 Ella crashed
3 We both forgot our
4 Get down from that wall or you'll
5 Dean had a little
6 My phone broke when I

a fall off and hurt yourself!
b her car into a post box this morning.
c accident on his bike, but he's fine.
d house keys this morning.
e some money from my wallet.
f dropped it on the ground.

physical actions

2 A Choose the correct word or phrase to complete the sentences.

1 You have to .... the door open, not push it.
   a jump   b climb   c pull
2 .... the link for more information.
   a Click on   b Point at   c Kick
3 The baby .... my finger but it didn't hurt.
   a climbed   b bit   c jumped
4 I need to .... the jam from the top shelf.
   a get   b point   c bite
5 Don't .... at that man, it's not nice!
   a click   b kick   c point
6 Can you hold this ladder while I .... it?
   a climb   b fall over   c jump

B Complete the advertisement with a verb in each gap. The first letter is given.

Fun run and more!

Are you feeling stressed? Or bored? Then, come and try our fun run. It's not a normal run and I'll tell you why. In our run, you have to ¹c............... up walls and ²j............... over the top of them. You have to ³k............... footballs across a field and ⁴p............... car wheels in front of you from one end of a park to the other. It's not easy. You might ⁵f............... over, or stop because you're tired, but don't worry. It's a team sport and your team will help you get up again and keep running.

Sounds like fun? ⁶C............... here to find out more.

GRAMMAR

present perfect simple (2)

3 A Choose the correct word or phrase to complete the sentences.

1 We .... haven't met our new neighbour.
   a still   b already   c yet
2 I've .... seen your brother outside the supermarket!
   a yet   b just   c still
3 Have you finished the TV series ....?
   a recently   b still   c yet
4 We've done a lot of fun things ....
   a just   b yet   c recently
5 I haven't heard about the new job ....
   a yet   b still   c already
6 I've .... cleaned the kitchen, so you don't need to.
   a still   b already   c not yet

B Complete the sentences about Stefan's 'to do' list. Today is 12th October.

Things to do before moving home

Get some boxes	●	3 September 12.22
Pack the things in the garage	●	12 October 14.52
Book a company to move my things	●	5 October 9.35
Give my new address to my friends	●	12 October 8.35
Speak to the water company.	○	Called twice, no answer
Tell my bank about the move	●	3 October 10.07
Pack things in the house	○	
Pay someone to clean the oven	○	Emailed company, waiting for reply

1 He's .... some boxes. (already)
2 He's .... the things in the garage. (just)
3 He's .... to move his things. (recently)
4 He's .... to his friends. (just)
5 He .... the water company. (still)
6 He's .... his bank about the move. (recently)
7 He .... the things in the house .... (yet)
8 He .... someone to clean the oven. (still)

6B

PRONUNCIATION

4A weak and strong forms: *have / has* | Underline the weak sounds in *have* and *has*. Circle the strong sounds.

1 Have you finished with your glass?
2 We haven't seen this film yet.
3 Has she had breakfast? Yes, she has.
4 He hasn't finished work yet.
5 Has Benji had an argument with Gio?
6 Have we moved yet? No, we haven't.

B 6.02 | Listen and check.

LISTENING

5A 6.03 | Listen to a conversation between friends. Number the problems (a–f) in the order you hear them.

a got angry messages from manager
b walked into someone on a bike
c forgot phone
d didn't get up on time
e dropped bag
f missed bus

B 6.03 | Listen again. Complete each sentence with a word, number or a time.

1 The man woke up at .... a.m.
2 Before the man left home, he put on clothes and brushed his ....
3 The man left home at .... a.m.
4 The man had to wait .... minutes for another bus.
5 The woman thinks it's .... that the man missed his bus stop.
6 The cyclist felt .... after the accident.
7 The man took a .... to a hospital.
8 The man was in the hospital for .... hours.
9 The man got home at .... p.m.
10 The man had .... messages from his manager on his phone.

C How did the man probably feel in each situation? Choose the correct word.

1 **interested / stressed** when he woke up
2 **angry / positive** when he missed his bus
3 **confident / worried** in the hospital
4 **afraid / pleased** when he found out his foot was OK
5 **happy / unhappy** when he saw his messages

D 6.04 | Listen to the recording. Write what you hear. You will hear the sentences only once.

1 ....
2 ....
3 ....
4 ....

WRITING

an informal email giving news

6A Read the email. What is Maya's news? Choose the correct options (a–e).

Hi Drew!

How are ¹............ ? I ²............ you're well.

A few things have happened here ³............ . I've ⁴............ finished my exams. I was really stressed about them, but I think they went well. Now I've got three months off before the new university year starts. I need some money so I've got a summer job in a restaurant. It's hard work, but I like the people there.

My other ⁵............ news is that I've finally got a car! Now I don't have to take two buses to town. It's brilliant. It's only a cheap car, but I love it because it's all mine.

That's ⁶............ my news for now. Say hello to everyone there ⁷............ .

All the ⁸............ ,

Maya

a She's got a car.
b She's moved to a new home.
c She's finished her exams.
d She's got a job.
e She's lost her job.

B Complete the email in Ex 6A with the words in the box.

| all | best | big | for me | hope |
| just | recently | things |

7A You are going to write a reply to Maya from Drew with Drew's news. Choose two or three pieces of news from below.

- forgot something important
- got a new job
- had an accident
- learnt a new skill
- lost something
- made a new friend
- moved home
- started a new hobby

B Plan your email. Decide these things.

- how to start your email
- the order of news
- useful phrases you can use
- how to end your email

C Write the email from Drew to Maya. Write 80–120 words.

Lesson 6C

HOW TO... | talk about health problems
VOCABULARY | health and illness; the body and symptoms
PRONUNCIATION | connected speech: final -t and -d

VOCABULARY

health and illness

1 Complete the information with the words in the box.

> emergency   medical   prescription   results
> surgery   symptoms   treatment   virus

In an ¹..................., call 999. Otherwise, for other ²................... problems, make an appointment to see a doctor.

Note down your ³................... so you can remember them when you visit the ⁴....................

Your doctor will listen to you and decide on the best ⁵..................., e.g. bed rest or painkillers. The doctor may decide you need more tests and wait for the ⁶................... of those.

When you need medicine, the doctor will give you a ⁷.................... Take this to a chemist's. Remember that when you have a ⁸................... like the flu, it's better not to visit your doctor because other people can become ill.

the body and symptoms

2 A Choose the correct word or phrase to complete the sentences.

1 I put some very hot food in my mouth and now my .... hurts.
   a toe   **b** tongue   **c** elbow
2 I can't move my head because I've got a ....
   a stiff neck   **b** temperature   **c** cough
3 I wear my watch on my right ....
   a toe   **b** lip   **c** wrist
4 I really hurt the little .... on my left hand yesterday.
   a ankle   **b** finger   **c** toe
5 My bag keeps falling off my ....
   a throat   **b** shoulder   **c** knee
6 I can't walk because my .... hurts.
   a ankle   **b** elbow   **c** lip

B Write the problem for each description. The first letter is given.

1 My teeth are very painful. t...................
2 My arm hurts when I bend it. a p................... e...................
3 My head hurts. h...................
4 It hurts when I speak. s................... t...................
5 My back hurts. b...................
6 I feel very hot – I'm 39°C. high t...................

How to ...

talk about health problems

3 A 🔊 6.05 | Listen to a conversation. What is the problem?

> backache   painful wrist   stiff neck   toothache   virus

B Use the prompts to make sentences.

1 how / help / you?
2 I / got / sore throat / and / can't stop / cough.
3 I feel / really tired / and dizzy / and / body / ache.
4 I / got / temperature / too.
5 when / these symptoms / start?
6 sound / like / you / got / virus.
7 should / stay / home.
8 mustn't / more than eight tablets / twenty-four hours.

C 🔊 6.05 | Listen again and check.

PRONUNCIATION

4 🔊 6.06 | connected speech: final -t and -d | Listen and choose the sentences where the speaker pronounces the -d or -t sound at the end of the words in bold.

1 I've **got** a stiff neck.
2 I've **hurt** my shoulder.
3 I've **put** ice on it.
4 I'm **worried** about my elbow.
5 You **shouldn't** go to work.
6 If you **don't** feel better soon, give me a call.

SPEAKING

5 A Complete the conversation with the words in the box.

> got   hurts   mustn't   painful
> put   should   taken   worried

Doctor: What can I do for you?
Patient: I'm ¹................... about my wrist. I fell over this morning. My wrist is really ²................... now. I can't move it.
Doctor: Let's have a look.
Patient: I've ³................... ice on it and ⁴................... some painkillers, but it still hurts a lot.
Doctor: It's possible that you've broken it. You ⁵................... get an X-ray.
Patient: Oh no! It's my writing hand, too.

B 🔊 6.07 | Listen and check.

C 🔊 6.08 | You are the patient in Ex 5A. Listen and speak after the beep. Record the conversation if you can.

D Listen to your recording and compare it to Ex 5B.

Speak anywhere   Go to the interactive speaking practice

Lesson 6D

GRAMMAR | *be* + adjective + *to* infinitive
READING | teenage pilots

GRAMMAR

be + adjective + *to* infinitive

1 A The sentences below have a mistake. Choose the best option to correct the mistake.

1 We're sorry <u>to hearing</u> about your accident.
   a hearing
   b hear
   c to hear
2 It's easy <u>sit</u> and do nothing all day!
   a sitting
   b to sitting
   c to sit
3 This game is too boring <u>of us to play</u>.
   a of us play
   b for us to play
   c for us play
4 Be careful <u>to not wake up</u> late.
   a to wake up not
   b not to wake up
   c to not waking up

B Complete the sentences with the words in brackets.

1 It's good .... (not / work) too hard.
2 It was kind .... (you / call) me yesterday.
3 It's important .... (not / get) too stressed.
4 I'm surprised .... (see) you here today.
5 It was really nice .... (you / help) yesterday.
6 I think it feels .... (safe / drive) in the day than at night.

READING

2 A Read the article. Complete the summary with one word or a number from the article in each gap.

A teenage girl and her [1]............... have each flown around the world on their own. Zara began her trip in [2]............... 2021. She stopped at [3]............... different places before she got arrived home in [4]............... 2022. Mack began his trip in [5]............... 2022 and arrived home in [6]............... 2022 after he went over [7]............... countries.

B Read the article again. Who is each sentence about: Zara (Z) or Mack (M)?

1 Who didn't start their journey in the country they live in?
2 Who didn't like flying over cold places?
3 Who experienced cold and storms?
4 Who spent one night in a place completely alone?
5 Who slept in an airport?
6 Who regularly talked to parents?
7 Who liked flying over Africa?
8 Who had other planes to welcome them home?

Teenage pilots fly around the world

Many teenagers dream of getting on a plane and travelling to another country. But what must it be like for a teenager to fly alone around the world in their own plane? That's what Mack and Zara Rutherford have done. The brother and sister are Belgian but have British parents. They are two of the youngest people to fly solo around the world in a light aeroplane. Zara, aged nineteen, was first. She left Belgium in August 2021 and returned in January 2022. Her trip involved sixty stops and took two months longer than she wanted because of stormy weather. She spent a month in the USA, where she used her time to apply for university. She slept in an airport in Indonesia for two days because she couldn't leave the airport. She had problems with her plane in New Mexico in the USA and Singapore, but she was most worried about flying across some of the coldest parts of the world, because her plane might stop working. When Zara arrived back in Belgium, four planes from the Belgian air force were there to meet her.

Zara's seventeen-year-old brother, Mack, left Sofia in Bulgaria in March 2022 and landed in the same place in August. He travelled across fifty-two countries and two oceans. He had problems with the hot weather in Dubai and closed airports in India. He also slept on an island in the Pacific where nobody lives. He enjoyed flying over national parks in Kenya and buildings in Manhattan, New York.

Mack spoke to his parents each day and got advice from his sister, too. Flying is important in the Rutherford family. Mack's parents are both pilots and his great-great grandmother was one of the first women in South Africa to fly a plane. Now that Mack is home, he isn't sure what he wants to do for a career, but he knows he wants to continue flying.

5-6 REVIEW

GRAMMAR

1 A Write a word to fill the gaps.

subject pronoun	possessive pronoun
I	mine
you	1 ....
2	ours
she	3 ....
4	his
they	5 ....

B Complete each sentence with a pronoun, *that*, *then* or *whose*.

1 .... is this phone? Is it Jan's?
2 This toy has lost .... head.
3 Have you seen my brother? I've got something for ....
4 I finish work at 6 p.m. I'll message you ....
5 You fell over in front of the class? Sorry, but ....'s really funny!
6 That glass is ...., not yours. I had my water in it.

2 Choose the correct word to complete the sentences.

1 Have you got **any / many / lots** apple juice?
2 There's **much / too much / too many** noise in here.
3 I need **a bit of / many / too much** time to finish this project.
4 Do we have **a bit of / enough / much** computers for everyone?
5 I'd love **any / enough / some** coffee.
6 We don't have **a lot of / many / some** money.
7 Would you like **enough / some / too much** lunch?
8 I'm **too / too many / too much** tired to go out tonight.

3 Put the words in the correct order to make sentences.

1 new boots? / me / Can / your / show / you
2 some / lent / Sofia / money. / I've
3 a leaving card / got / for Zack. / We've
4 passed / I've / to Maggie. / your email address
5 question. / me / asked / interesting / Naomi / an
6 all our customers / a short / I / to / email / sent
7 your / you / the woman / Did / name? / tell
8 for / Shall I / some flowers / mum? / your / buy

4 Put the words in brackets in the correct place in the sentences (1–6). Change the form of the words when necessary.

How to stop feeling stressed

We all experience some stress in our lives. A little stress is fine, but a lot of stress can be a problem. So, how can we stop this? Here are some tips.

- Get outside and do some exercise. ¹You don't have to .... run .... around a field (fast). A short walk can help.

- Do exercise with other people. ²I .... go the gym .... with a friend twice a week (normal). We do exercise and chat.

- ³Try to .... eat .... (healthy). Have a few of the unhealthy things you like but not a lot.

- Plan your day. Before, I tried to do too much. ⁴It often .... went .... (bad). It made me feel really stressed.

- Try to arrive early to things. ⁵I was so busy that I was .... late .... for meetings and appointments (often). That made my stress worse.

- Help other people. ⁶I .... don't .... have time to do this (always). But I try, because it makes me feel good and that takes away some stress.

5 Use the prompts in brackets to complete the conversation.

A: (you / book / the meeting room for tomorrow / yet)
1 ....?
B: No, not yet. I haven't had time.
A: Have you invited everyone?
B: Yes. (I / just / send / them all an invitation)
2 ....
A: Great, thanks.
B: (Ed / already / reply)
3 ....
A: Good. What did he say?
B: He can't come because he'll be on holiday tomorrow.
A: Oh, right. It's an important meeting.
B: I know, but (he / not / have / any holidays this year / yet)
4 ....
A: Hmm.
B: He's going away next week. (He / already / pay for / a flight and hotel)
5 ....
A: OK, fine, but (he / still / not / finish / last month's report) He promised it days ago.
6 ....

44

REVIEW 5-6

6 Add one word to each sentence.
1 It's hard understand Max sometimes.
2 It was really nice you to drive me home.
3 It exciting to think of living in another country.
4 It was wrong me to get angry – I'm sorry.
5 It's better get up early than to go to bed late.
6 Be careful to leave the oven on – you don't want to start a fire.

VOCABULARY

7 Choose the correct word to complete the sentences.
1 This dish is old and very **fair** / **valuable**.
2 I've spent all my money **for** / **on** a new phone.
3 Let's **cost** / **rent** some bikes and go cycling.
4 I paid a **fair** / **fine** price for these shoes.
5 We've had a few **offers** / **savings** for our business.
6 The price of milk has **increased** / **go up**.
7 This suit **bought** / **cost** a lot of money!
8 I've got quite a lot of **savings** / **spending** in my bank.

8 Match the countable nouns in the box with the uncountable nouns (1–10).

apartment   battery   chair   jumper   lorry
meal   post   suggestion   suitcase   word

1 accommodation   6 furniture
2 advice   7 luggage
3 electricity   8 social media
4 fashion   9 traffic
5 food   10 vocabulary

9 Complete the sentences with an adjective. The first letter is given.
1 This room is long and n............... Can we fit a bed in?
2 There's no coffee in the pot. It's e................. .
3 The light in here is very b................. .
4 Is that a metal spoon or a p................. one?
5 Touch this jumper. It's so s.................!
6 Your hair's w................. from the rain.

10 Complete the sentences with *did*, *played* or *went* and a sport in the box.

athletics   cricket   sailing   skiing   table tennis   yoga

1 The man hit a ball with a piece of wood and then ran to a place and back as many times as possible. He ....
2 The woman stood on two pieces of wood and travelled down a mountain. She ....
3 The man lay on the floor and did slow exercises to relax. He ....
4 The man hit a small ball across a low net on a small table. He ....
5 The woman ran 100 metres. Then she ran and jumped as far as she could. She ....
6 The woman travelled across the water on a boat. She ....

11 Complete the social media conversation with the words in the box.

argument   bit   climbed   crashed   dropped
fell off   forgot   get   pulled   took

How was your weekend?

> Busy! We had a party for my son Alfie in our garden. It's his birthday.

How was it?

> Well, we didn't stop once. One boy ¹............... onto a table. He then ²............... and hurt his knee. A girl was cycling around on her bike. She ³............... into a tree.

I hope they're OK.

> Yeah, they were fine. Alfie tried to ⁴............... a toy down from the top shelf in his bedroom and ⁵............... the whole shelf down on top of him.

Oh dear!

> A boy and girl had an ⁶............... . The girl ⁷............... to bring a gift for Alfie so she ⁸............... the boy's gift instead! While she was giving it back, she ⁹............... it and it broke.

Oh my goodness!

> And finally, a girl ¹⁰............... the cake before we gave it to Alfie because she was hungry.

😂

> And that was just in the first twenty minutes!

😂😂😂

12 Complete the sentences. The first letter of each word is given.
1 I need a p............... for some strong painkillers.
2 I've got a really s............... throat this morning.
3 I feel d............... when I stand up.
4 I get p............... knees when I sit for a long time.
5 I've got a stomach a............... from all the food I ate.
6 I'm waiting for some test r............... from the surgery.

Lesson 7A

GRAMMAR | present continuous with future reference; other future forms
VOCABULARY | going out and staying in
PRONUNCIATION | linking /j/, /w/ and /r/

VOCABULARY

going out and staying in

1 A Choose the correct word or phrase to complete the sentences.

1 I .... a really good programme last night.
   a had   **b** went   **c** watched

2 Do you want to .... on a tour when we visit Berlin?
   a go to   **b** go   **c** have

3 Let's .... an evening out.
   a go to   **b** have   **c** go

4 Shall we .... the market to buy bread?
   a go   **b** go to   **c** see

5 We're going to .... my brother's band play.
   a see   **b** go   **c** go to

6 We're .... out with friends tomorrow night.
   a seeing   **b** going to   **c** going

B Complete the article with the words in the box.

> a basketball game   a film   a meal out
> a night in   for a coffee   some friends round
> some live music   to the theatre

Fun activities for staying in or going out

How do you prefer to spend your free evenings? Do you like to have ¹............... so you can sit in front of the TV and watch a programme or two? Or do you prefer to have ²............... at a restaurant, or see ³............... at the cinema? Whether you stay in or go out, there are always fun things to do. For example, you can stay at home and see ⁴................ Yes, you can watch your favourite band using virtual reality (VR). Or if you prefer sport, you can watch ⁵............... or any other sport using VR. You could also have ⁶............... to your home and do an online escape room together. That's a game where you have sixty minutes to find clues and solve problems to win.

If you prefer to go out, you could go ⁷............... to see a play. If you want a quieter time, you could find an unusual place to go ⁸..............., like a café in a treehouse!

PRONUNCIATION

2 🔊 **7.01** | linking /j/, /w/ and /r/ | Choose the correct sound to link each pair of words in bold. Then listen and check.

1 Let's **see a** film.   /j/ / /w/ / /r/
2 I'd like to go **for a** coffee   /j/ / /w/ / /r/
3 Can we **go on** a bus tour?   /j/ / /w/ / /r/
4 We need to go **to a** market.   /j/ / /w/ / /r/
5 Shall we **see a** show?   /j/ / /w/ / /r/

GRAMMAR

present continuous with future reference; other future forms

3 A The sentences below have a mistake. Choose the best option to correct the mistake.

1 I <u>meet</u> Dave outside the cinema at eight.
   a 'll meeting   **b** 'm going meet   **c** 'm meeting

2 Is Rob <u>going to moving</u> abroad soon?
   a go to move   **b** go to move   **c** going to move

3 Did Julio just call? I <u>going to ring</u> him straightaway.
   a 'm ringing   **b** 'll ring   **c** ring

4 We're moving to a new office <u>on a month</u> time.
   a on a months   **b** in a months   **c** in a month's time

B Choose ALL the correct verb forms.

1 I'm **going to meet** / **meeting** / **meet** up with Sara later today.

2 Is that the doorbell? I **'m going to get** / **'m getting** / **'ll get** it!

3 It's hot in here. **Am I opening** / **Will I** / **Shall I** open a window?

4 We **'re going to see** / **'re seeing** / **seeing** a band tomorrow night. Do you want to come?

5 Martyn's coming to see us **at** / **in** / **on** a few days.

C Complete the conversation with the correct future form of the verbs in brackets. Use the present continuous, 'll or shall.

What are you doing tonight?

I ¹............... (have) a night in. I'm tired. You?

I ²............... (go) out with some friends. I thought you might want to come.

I don't know. Where ³............... (you / go)?

We ⁴............... (have) a meal at Franky's first. Then we ⁵............... (go) to Club Dance.

Oh, I haven't been there for ages. OK, I ⁶............... (come). I can sleep tomorrow!

Great! We ⁷............... (meet) at Franky's at 9. ⁸............... (I / get) my taxi to pick you up?

No, it's OK. I ⁹............... (get) the bus into town. I ¹⁰............... (see) you at the restaurant.

LISTENING

4 A 🔊 **7.02** | Listen to Marcus's conversations with his friends (1–4). Choose the best response (a or b) to continue each conversation.

1. a What's the name of the restaurant?
   b I know the one you mean. It's on Wells Street.
2. a The live music is the best thing about a show.
   b You're a great singer. You could be an actress.
3. a How are you getting there? Are you driving?
   b The shopping centre nearest to my house closes at seven on a Friday.
4. a I haven't seen that crime show yet.
   b I wanted to have a night out with my friends, but you're all busy!

B 🔊 **7.02** | Listen again and choose the correct words.

1. Jake's going to his **nephew's / niece's** birthday party.
2. Jake's looking forward to the **food / games** at the party.
3. Zara's going to the theatre with **family / colleagues**.
4. Zara **has / hasn't** seen the show before.
5. Flavia and her sister need to buy **dresses / gifts** for a wedding.
6. The shopping centre is **sixteen / sixty** minutes from where Flavia is now.
7. Jimi thinks Emi has a **cold / flu**.
8. Jimi is excited about a new **film / TV programme**.

C 📝 🔊 **7.03** | Listen to the recording. Write what you hear. You will hear the sentences only once.

1. ....
2. ....
3. ....
4. ....

WRITING

an email making arrangements

5 A Complete the email with the present continuous form of the verbs in brackets.

Hi!

I'm so excited about your visit. What time does your plane land? How ¹.................. (you / get) from the airport to my house? Shall I meet you there?

I've made a few plans for us for Tuesday and Wednesday. I hope that's OK. On Tuesday morning, we ².................. (go) sightseeing. I've booked us a river tour! Then, we ³.................. (visit) the market in the old part of the town. I love it there. On Wednesday, we ⁴.................. (see) a comedy show. It's with local actors. It'll be really funny and I think you'll like it.

I know you've made some arrangements for Thursday and Friday. Am I included? I hope so.

Can't wait to see you!

Liv

B Read the email again. Are the statements True (T) or False (F)?

1. Liv has made an arrangement to meet you at the airport.
2. Liv has made arrangements for two days of your trip.
3. Liv has bought tickets for a tour of the market.
4. The market is in the modern part of the town.
5. You're going to see a local comedy show.
6. Liv wants to be part of your plans for Thursday and Friday.

6 A You are going to write a reply to Liv. Use the prompts to make sentences about your arrangements. Use the present continuous.

1. I / take / taxi / Liv's house
2. We / rent / bikes / to go to Epson Forest / Thursday morning
3. We / have / meal out / Thursday evening
4. I / go / shopping / Friday

My trip

Arrive: 14.15. Taxi booked to Liv's house

Thursday arrangements for me and Liv
Morning – rent bikes – Epson Forest
Evening – meal out. Booked new seafood restaurant

Friday plans for me (and Liv?)
Shopping – birthday gift for Mum

B Plan your email. Decide these things.

- how to start your email
- what to say about your arrival at Liv's house
- what to say about Liv meeting you at the train station
- what to say about your arrangements for Thursday and Friday
- how to end your email

C Write the email to Liv. Write 80–120 words.

Lesson 7B

GRAMMAR | indefinite pronouns: *someone, nothing, anywhere,* etc.
VOCABULARY | eating out and eating in; containers
PRONUNCIATION | sentence stress with indefinite pronouns

VOCABULARY

eating out and eating in

1 Complete the social media post with the words in the box.

> containers   deliver   delivery   order
> pick up   takeaway   tip   used

Last night, my flatmate and I decided to get an Indian ¹............ from our local restaurant. We ²............ their app to look at their menu and ³............ the food. The restaurant isn't far away and it's possible for us to ⁴............ our meals, but we're a bit lazy and we always ask them to ⁵............ them! Anyway, the food arrived about thirty minutes later and we gave the delivery man a £3 ⁶............ and thanked him. When we opened the bags, we found it wasn't our order. We called the restaurant and they told us we could have it. Lucky us, because there were more dishes and they were nicer than the cheap ones we usually had! In fact, it was probably the best ⁷............ service we've ever had! So, we ate it and enjoyed it all. This morning, I was putting the empty food ⁸............ in the recycling bin when I saw my neighbour. Of course, I told him all about the amazing food we had. I even invited him to come the restaurant with me and my flatmate one day!

containers

2A Choose the correct word to complete the sentences.

1 Can you open this .... of jam for me?
  a jar **b** bottle **c** can
2 Whose is this .... of cereal in the kitchen?
  a mug **b** pot **c** bowl
3 I need to buy a new .... of toothpaste.
  a tube **b** tin **c** carton
4 I just bought Annie a .... of chocolates.
  a carton **b** box **c** pot
5 I'm going to make us all a .... of tea.
  a jar **b** tin **c** mug
6 I can't believe Sami ate the last .... of crisps!
  a packet **b** carton **c** pot

B Choose the odd item out.

1 a pot of: **coffee** / **honey** / **crisps** / **tea**
2 a tin of: **beans** / **butter** / **peas** / **tomatoes**
3 a bottle of: **juice** / **soda** / **soup** / **water**
4 a bowl of: **fruit** / **pasta** / **rice** / **sandwiches**
5 a mug of: **cake** / **coffee** / **hot chocolate** / **soup**

GRAMMAR

indefinite pronouns: *someone, nothing, anywhere,* etc.

3A Choose the correct word to complete the sentences.

1 .... has arrived so we can start eating.
  a No one **b** Everyone **c** Someone
2 There's .... to buy clothes around here.
  a nowhere **b** everywhere **c** somewhere
3 I ordered pasta, but the waiter brought me .... different.
  a nothing **b** everything **c** something
4 Hello, is there .... here?
  a nobody **b** everybody **c** anybody
5 When the box arrived, there wasn't .... in it!
  a nothing **b** anything **c** something
6 There's nothing .... in the fridge.
  a eat **b** to eat **c** eating

B Complete the conversations with indefinite pronouns. Use *some-, any-, no-* and *-thing, -one, -where*.

A: Would you like something to eat?
B: No, ¹............, thanks. I had ²............ earlier.
A: What about a drink? We haven't got ³............ particularly special, but we have got some juice.
B: I'd love a glass of apple juice if you have it.
A: Oh! There was apple juice here. I think ⁴............ has drunk it.
B: Perfect, thanks!

A: I can't find my keys ⁵............. I usually put them in the dish over there when I get home. Maybe ⁶............ moved them.
B: I haven't touched them and there's ⁷............ else here, so I don't think ⁸............ has moved them.
A: Can you help me look for them?
B: Where do you want to look?
A: ⁹............! I need to leave soon.
B: Sure. Wait, what have you got in your hand?
A: There's ¹⁰............ in my hand ... Oh! My keys!

PRONUNCIATION

4A 🔊 7.04 | sentence stress with indefinite pronouns | Listen and complete the sentences.

1 Is there .... to eat in the kitchen?
2 There's .... for me to sit.
3 I don't have .... to do tomorrow.
4 I'm bored. I need .... to do.
5 There's .... enough to help me lift these boxes.

B Choose the correct words to complete the rule.

The indefinite pronouns are ¹**stressed** / **unstressed**.
The adjectives are ²**stressed** / **unstressed**.

READING

5 A Read the article and choose the main topic (a–c).
   a How delivery riders can stay safe in their jobs
   b A day in the life of a fast-food delivery rider
   c The advantages and disadvantages of being a delivery rider

What's it like to deliver someone else's takeaway?

You pick up your phone, open the app, select your order and wait for your takeaway to arrive. But do you ever think about the life of the delivery person who brings it? What is it like to deliver food?

I'm a university student and also a delivery rider. Between Friday and Sunday evening, I cycle up to 150 km delivering food to people in my area. It can be a difficult job, and dangerous, but it can also be fun. You need to be fit and healthy. It's not always about cycling as quickly as possible. When you're carrying soup or hot coffee, it's not a good idea to go very fast. You need to think about staying safe on the roads and in traffic, too. So, it's about good cycling and safety skills, not speed. You need to follow directions, so if you can't use a map app then it might not be the job for you. It's also good to know the area, because then you know all the shorter routes to take and that saves you time. More time means more opportunities to deliver more food. And that means more pay.

The delivery company pays me for every order I take from a restaurant or café to a customer. It doesn't pay me for every hour I work. This is both good and bad. On the positive side, I can decide when I work and it is possible to make quite good money. On the negative side, I don't get paid well when it's quiet and there aren't many orders. That's why I work at the weekends. It's always busy. Another negative is that I don't get sick pay. If I feel unwell and don't work, I don't get paid.

However, there are many things I like about my Friday-to-Sunday job. It's wonderful to be outdoors and not at a desk or in a hot kitchen, for example. It's also quite easy. I just use the company's app on my phone to see what orders I have to deliver. I've made some friends with the other riders and I know they'll help me when I need to repair my bike. I chat to restaurant workers and customers, but these are short, pleasant conversations. For the rest of the time, I can enjoy the sun on my face and the fresh air. (Of course, sometimes there's rain pouring down my back, but let's not talk about that!)

Being a delivery rider isn't for everyone, but it works for me because I love working outdoors and being on my bike for a few days each week. I get to do my hobby while working.

B Read the article again and choose the correct option (a–c) to complete the sentences.

1 The writer says that to be a good delivery rider
   a you must know an area very well.
   b you must cycle very quickly.
   c you must know how to cycle safely.
2 One problem with being a delivery rider is that
   a you only get paid for deliveries you make.
   b work gets too busy at the weekends.
   c it can make you ill.
3 One good thing about being a delivery rider is that
   a you get to spend a lot of time with other people.
   b your company fixes your bike if it stops working.
   c there's no need to spend your working day inside.
4 The writer says the job is good for him because
   a he makes a lot of money.
   b he loves being on his bike.
   c he loves all types of weather.

C Complete each sentence with a word or number from the article.

1 The writer starts work each week on a ....
2 The writer can cycle .... km a week.
3 One food the writer says he carries is ....
4 The writer saves time when he knows quicker .... to take.
5 The writer works at the weekends because they're ....
6 The writer uses the company's .... to see his orders.
7 The writer talks to ...., restaurant workers and other riders.
8 The writer enjoys feeling the .... when he's out cycling.

Lesson 7C

HOW TO ... | ask for and give permission
VOCABULARY | permission
PRONUNCIATION | polite intonation when asking permission

VOCABULARY

permission

1 A Choose the correct word or phrase to complete the sentences.

1 They _____ the use of cameras at the museum.
   a 've banned   b mustn't touch   c can't take off
2 You _____ any of the things in the museum.
   a shouldn't lean   b don't let   c mustn't touch
3 The museum _____ smoking inside.
   a can't take off   b doesn't allow   c shouldn't lean
4 They _____ you take backpacks into the museum.
   a can't take off   b mustn't touch   c don't let
5 You _____ on the walls near the paintings.
   a shouldn't lean   b mustn't touch   c don't allow
6 I'm afraid you _____ your coats in here.
   a can't take off   b 've banned   c don't let

B Complete the second sentence so that it has a similar meaning to the first. Use the words in brackets.

1 You're not allowed to touch that.
  You _____ that. (mustn't)
2 I'm sorry, but you have to wait in a different place.
  I'm sorry, but you _____ in here. (can't)
3 You're not allowed to have pets here.
  They _____ have pets here. (let)
4 It's not a good idea to stand against the window.
  You _____ against the window. (lean)
5 You need to keep your coat on – you can't carry it.
  You _____ your coat or carry it. (take)

How to ...

ask for and give permission

2 A 🔊 7.05 | Listen to four conversations (1–4). Match each one to the locations (a–d).

   a a library
   b someone's home
   c a museum
   d an office

B 🔊 7.05 | Listen again. Choose the correct words to complete the sentences.

1 In Conversation 1, the man said it was **fine** / **not fine** for the woman to use her camera in this room.
2 In Conversation 2, the woman said it was **OK** / **not OK** for the students to use the room to discuss their project.
3 In Conversation 3, the man said it was **fine** / **not fine** for the woman to enter the meeting room.
4 In Conversation 4, the woman said it was fine for the man to take **any** / **most** food from the fridge.

C 🔊 7.06 | Add a word to each sentence or delete one word. Then listen and check.

1 Excuse me, is it OK I take a photo in here?
2 I'm a sorry, you can't.
3 It all right if we discuss our project in here?
4 Sure, no problem, but you shouldn't to talk loudly.
5 Well, can we to use that room over there instead?
6 I'm afraid that's possible.
7 May I to come in?
8 I'm afraid.
9 You can to help yourself to food in the fridge while you're staying with us.
10 You do mustn't eat Jack's yoghurts.

PRONUNCIATION

3 🔊 7.07 | **polite intonation when asking permission** | Listen and decide if the intonation is polite (P) or not polite (N).

1 P / N   4 P / N
2 P / N   5 P / N
3 P / N   6 P / N

SPEAKING

4 A Complete the conversation with the words in the box.

| afraid   can   can't   may   OK |
| problem   shouldn't   think |

A: Hello!
B: Hello. Is it ¹_____ if I sit on the floor here? I'd like to draw a copy of the painting there.
A: I'm ²_____ that's not possible. People walk through here. They might fall over you.
B: Right. Well, ³_____ I sit on that chair over there?
A: I'm sorry, you ⁴_____. It's actually a 200-year-old chair. You ⁵_____ sit on my chair here. I'm happy to stand for a bit.
B: That's kind of you, thanks. Do you ⁶_____ I could move it over there?
A: Sure, no ⁷_____. You ⁸_____ take too long to draw your picture, though. The museum closes in forty minutes.
B: That's fine. I draw fast!

B 🔊 7.08 | Listen and check.

C 🔊 7.09 | You are B in Ex 4A. Listen and speak after the beep. Record the conversation if you can.

D Listen to your recording and compare it to Ex 4B.

Lesson 7D

GRAMMAR | adverbial and prepositional phrases
LISTENING | talk about an important photo

GRAMMAR

adverbial and prepositional phrases

1 A Choose the correct word or phrase to complete the sentences.

1 Stand .... of the tree, not behind it!
   a background **b** in front **c** middle
2 I'm on the right-hand .... of the photo.
   a side **b** end **c** front
3 Look, you can see the sea in the ....
   a left **b** middle of **c** distance
4 The children are standing .... park.
   a in a **b** of a **c** at a
5 My parents are in the .... the picture.
   a right **b** background **c** middle of
6 Eve's the woman .... grey hair.
   a with **b** of **c** for

B Look at the photo. Complete the sentences with *front*, *with* or *without*.

1 Andre is the man .... glasses.
2 The friends are in .... of a fairly modern building.
3 Yu is the woman .... the phone camera.
4 Luca and Yu are the ones .... glasses.
5 All the friends are looking at the camera .... a smile.

C Look at the photo and use the prompts to make sentences.

1 Meera and Yu / are / middle / the photo
2 Yu / is / front / Meera
3 Andre / is / left / the photo
4 Luca / is / right-hand / side / the photo
5 Meera / is / back / the group of friends
6 background / there is / a building

LISTENING

2 A 🔊 **7.10** | Listen to part of a radio programme called *A photo that changed my life*. How did a photo change the man's life? Choose the correct option.

a He met an important person.
b He found a new home.
c He earned a lot of money.

B 🔊 **7.10** | Listen again and choose the correct option (a–c) to answer the questions.

1 What part of the photo interested Aiden the most?
   a The waterfall
   b The sky
   c The mountain
2 Where did Aiden see the photo?
   a A friend sent it to him.
   b He saw it on social media.
   c It was in a magazine.
3 How did Aiden get the money to visit Iceland?
   a He worked and saved money.
   b He used money he got as a gift.
   c He borrowed money from his parents.
4 How did Aiden feel when he got to Iceland?
   a nervous
   b excited
   c calm
5 How did Aiden find a job?
   a He answered a newspaper job advertisement.
   b He learnt about it from someone he talked to.
   c He saw an article about it on a website.
6 How often does Aiden see his family?
   a Once a year
   b Twice a year
   c Three times a year

C 🔊 **7.11** | Listen to the recording. Write what you hear. You will hear the sentences only once.

1 ....
2 ....
3 ....
4 ....

Lesson 8A

GRAMMAR | *will* for predictions
VOCABULARY | change
PRONUNCIATION | contractions: *'ll* and *won't*

VOCABULARY

change

1 A Complete the table with the phrases in the box.

> become fitter   become cheaper
> get faster   get smaller   go down
> improve   increase   stay the same

become more or better	become less or worse	no change

B Choose the correct word or phrase to complete the sentences.

1 The price of meat is .... up a lot.
   a staying   **b** going   **c** becoming
2 The .... of change in technology in the last ten years has been very fast.
   a activity   **b** same   **c** speed
3 I run in the park every day and I'm ....
   a going up   **b** increasing   **c** getting faster
4 My memory is terrible and it's getting ....
   a better   **b** worse   **c** the same
5 We've all changed but my brother hasn't. He has .... the same.
   a gone down   **b** stayed   **c** improved
6 Mobile phone technology has .... a lot in the last twenty years.
   a improved   **b** increased   **c** gone up

C Use the words in brackets to complete the text. Change the form of the words if necessary.

> Mobile phone technology is ¹............ (get / good) all the time, so each year phones are ²............ (become / small) and thinner and so on. However, the ³............ (speed / change) is slower than it was. Yes, phones are still ⁴............ (improve), but the changes are smaller. And prices aren't ⁵............ (go / down). They're not even ⁶............ (stay / same). The prices of new phones are ⁷............ (increase) quite a lot. This means that we're paying a higher price for smaller improvements.

GRAMMAR

***will* for predictions**

2 A The sentences below have a mistake. Choose the best option to correct the mistake.

1 I'm sure Tom <u>is</u> late tomorrow as usual!
   a will being   **b** will be   **c** will been
2 Phones in 2030 <u>look</u> different to phones now.
   a will look   **b** will looking   **c** don't look
3 I don't <u>think I</u> get the job.
   a think I'll   **b** I think   **c** think I won't
4 We <u>probably don't</u> see you until nine o'clock tomorrow.
   a will probably   **b** won't probably   **c** probably won't

B Complete the forum posts. Use the prompts and the correct form of *will*.

Will we have mobile phones in the future?

Harry
¹............ (perhaps / we / all / have) smart watches or something similar. ²............ (we / wear) them on our wrists.

Abby
³............ (we / want) mobile phones in the future? Maybe we won't have them. We ⁴............ (spend) our time talking to people face-to-face like people did in the past!

Jak
I think phone batteries ⁵............ (last) a lot longer. I mean, days or weeks, which will make life much easier for us all!

Cam
@Jak I ⁶............ (not / think / we / have to / worry) about batteries at all. Technology will improve a lot so new batteries ⁷............ (last) forever.

PRONUNCIATION

3 🔊 **8.01** | contractions: *'ll* and *won't* | Listen and write the word you hear.

1 Everyone in the world .... have a smart phone.
2 He .... be here a bit later.
3 Summer temperatures .... get hotter.
4 It .... get any worse.
5 People .... have better phones.
6 I'm sure you .... feel better tomorrow.

READING

4 A Read articles A and B. Choose the correct statement (1–3).

1. The articles are on the same topic.
2. The articles are on similar but different topics.
3. The articles are on very different topics.

B Read the articles again. Complete the table with the different uses of social robots in the box.

at events   in hospitals   in museums
in office receptions   in shops
with children   with older people

mentioned in article A	mentioned in article B	mentioned in both articles

C Complete the sentences with one or two words from the articles.

1. A social robot might take you to the .... you want in a building.
2. A social robot might .... visitors to a shop.
3. A social robot can find out about a person's .... when they arrive at a hospital.
4. Social robots will talk to patients so they feel .... when they're in hospital.
5. Social robots can stop patients from feeling .... at a hospital.
6. Social robots can help children with learning difficulties to .... people.
7. Social robots can help children with their ....
8. Social robots can teach visitors about things they see in ....
9. A social robot can help older people to feel less ....
10. Twenty percent of young children believe that their .... will be a robot.

A The future use of social robots

'Social robots' are robots which can talk to us and talk to each other. Here's where we might see them in the future.

Business
When you go to an event, a shop or a shopping centre, a social robot might welcome you and give you information. It'll also answer any questions you might have.

Healthcare
Social robots can help busy hospital doctors and nurses by taking a patient's information when they first arrive at the hospital. For example, the robots can find out about a patient's medical history. They can chat to the patients to help them feel less worried.

Education
Already, social robots are working with children who have learning difficulties. The robots teach the children how to talk to other people. Research tells us the robots have been very successful doing this, so we will probably see many more of these types of robots in the future.

Friendships
Social robots could play a big part in the lives of some people, particularly older people who live alone and feel lonely. The robots will give older people someone to talk to. Imagine having long conversations about life with the digital assistant on your phone. It'll be similar to this.

Will we all have a social robot friend? Maybe not, but we will definitely see more social robots in the future.

B The future use of social robots

'Social robots' are robots which can talk to us and talk to each other. Here's where we might see them in the future.

Business
When you enter an office building, you might not see a person at the reception desk. You might see a social robot instead. The robot will welcome you, give you information about the company and answer your questions. It might even show you to the room you need.

Healthcare
Medical care isn't just about finding out what's wrong with a patient and giving them the right medicine. It's about helping the patient to stay positive in difficult times. Social robots could talk to patients during their stay in hospital. They could tell stories and jokes, to help the patients stay calm.

Education
Social robots can speak lots of different languages, which means they can work with children around the world. They can be a tutor for children who need extra help with their studies. They can also work in museums, teaching visitors – young and old – about the things there.

Friendships
In a study of 1,246 children aged 5–11, twenty percent of them said they think they'll have a robot best friend in the future. Social robots can play games with children and help to look after them.

Will we all have a social robot friend? Maybe not, but we will definitely see more social robots in the future.

Lesson 8B

GRAMMAR | first conditional
VOCABULARY | attitudes
PRONUNCIATION | linking in conditionals

VOCABULARY

attitudes

1 Are the phrases (1–8) positive (+) or negative (–)?
1 hope you have a good day
2 have a dream for the future
3 fail your driving test
4 have some work experience
5 worry about the future
6 look on the bright side
7 be impossible to do
8 always see the negative side

2 A Choose the correct word or phrase to complete the sentences.
1 Try not to .... about your exam tomorrow.
  a fail   b hope   c worry
2 Is it your .... to go to university?
  a worry   b experience   c dream
3 I don't have much .... of this type of work.
  a experience   b dream   c bright side
4 It's .... to understand this maths question.
  a negative   b bright   c impossible
5 We weren't successful but let's .... on the bright side.
  a hope   b look   c see
6 I .... everything goes well tomorrow.
  a hope   b see   c worry

B Complete the social media post with the words in the box.

bright side   dream   experience   failed
hope   impossible   negative side   worry

If at first you don't succeed …

I started my own business six years ago. I had a ¹............ to become really successful and make millions! But it's almost ²............ to make any money in the first year or two of a new business. I made some bad decisions and the business ³............ . I was really sad for a few months and I could only see the ⁴............ of having a business. However, after a while, I decided to look on the ⁵............ and be positive. I realised that I had a lot of ⁶............ from that business and I used it to start a new one. Now, I don't have millions, but my new business is going well so far. I ⁷............ about making mistakes again, but I ⁸............ that I will continue to be successful.

GRAMMAR

first conditional

3 A The sentences below have a mistake. Choose the best option to correct the mistake.
1 If you give me the money, I go and pay.
  a I'm going   b I'll going   c I'll go
2 We'll take you to the station if you wants.
  a want   b 've wanted   c 'll want
3 What we do if it rains tomorrow?
  a do we will   b do we   c will we do
4 If I not win the race, I'll be a bit angry.
  a doesn't win   b won't win   c don't win

B Complete the email to Luke with the correct form of the verbs in brackets. Use *will* or *won't*.

Hi!
I'm trying to make some life decisions and need your help! Here are the problems.
• My job has become boring. It's too easy.
• I really want to move to the city, but flats are expensive.
• I have problems sleeping. I always feel tired.
• I never have the energy for exercise and I don't feel very fit.
• My car is old and keeps breaking down. I can't afford a new one.

I feel stressed all the time, because of these problems! What's your advice?
Luke

Hi Luke,
It's great that you want to make some changes in your life. It sounds like you need a new job. If you ¹............ (look) at the websites for local newspapers, you ²............ (see) job advertisements there. And if you ³............ (talk) to your cousin Macy, she ⁴............ (help) you find something. She knows a lot of businesses in the city.
Have you thought about sharing a flat in the city with someone else? It ⁵............ (be) cheaper if you ⁶............ (share) the rent. Also, you ⁷............ (not / need) a car if you ⁸............ (move) into the city.
I think you can't sleep because you're stressed about your job, flat and car. You ⁹............ (feel) more relaxed if you ¹⁰............ (change) these things. If you ¹¹............ (feel) more relaxed, you ¹²............ (sleep) better. And if you ¹³............ (sleep) better, you ¹⁴............ (have) more energy for exercise. So, spend time on finding a job and flat.
I hope that helps! Good luck.
Esma

PRONUNCIATION

4 A 8.02 | linking in conditionals | Listen and complete the sentences with the words you hear.
1. I'll come out tonight if I'm not too tired.
2. _____ tomorrow, we won't go out.
3. I don't want to get a taxi _____.
4. I'll see you tomorrow _____.
5. _____ later, I'll let you know.
6. _____, we'll go to the beach.

B Put the links between the words in the gaps in Ex 4A.

I'll come out tonight if‿I'm not too tired.

LISTENING

5 A 8.03 | Listen to the introduction to a radio interview. What is the topic?
a How to start a successful business
b Different types of careers
c Different ways of thinking about life

B 8.04 | Listen to the first part of the interview. Choose the correct option (a or b) to complete the definitions.
1 An optimist is a person who
  a believes good things will happen.
  b works hard to be successful.
2 A pessimist is a person who
  a doesn't work hard, but is still successful.
  b expects bad things to happen.

6 A 8.05 | Listen to the rest of the interview. Choose the statement (a–c) that the doctor believes.
a Most people are optimists.
b Most people are pessimists.
c We are all both optimists and pessimists.

B 8.05 | Listen again. Match the words and phrases (1–8) with the type of person: optimist (O), pessimist (P) or both (B).
1 relaxed
2 excited to do activities
3 careful
4 do dangerous things
5 not surprised when things go wrong
6 surprised when things go wrong

C 8.06 | Listen to parts of the interview. Choose the correct definitions of the words and phrase below.
1 *motivated*
  a bored with an activity
  b excited to do an activity
2 *possible dangers*
  a the possibility that something bad will happen
  b the possibility that someone will do something bad
3 *shocked*
  a pleased by something good
  b surprised by something bad

WRITING

an advice post

7 A Read the problems (A and B). Then read the advice from voxpop22. Which problem is the advice for?

Kenny
I started work at my company three years ago. I am a very good worker and always do my best. However, the problem is that people don't seem to understand how hard I work. People who came to the company after me are now in higher positions and making more money than me. Should I stop working so hard? Or should I talk to someone about this?

Bluebell
My company has offered me my dream job. It's exactly what I want to do for more money than I get now. But I have to move to a city abroad. I'm very close to my family here and I'll miss them a lot. I haven't told them yet. What should I do?

voxpop22
It's difficult. If you take the job, you'll do work you love, but ¹_____ time with your family. If you stay, you'll see your family, but ²_____ an amazing job opportunity.

³_____ asking your family what they think? They might want to come and visit you in your new home! And if you ⁴_____ but they can't visit, you'll still have the chance to see your family online. What will happen if you don't like the job? Will it be possible to return to your old job? ⁵_____ talk to your manager and ask if this is possible. Then you can try the new job for six months and see.

👍 2 👎

B Complete the advice post with the phrases (a–e).
a You should
b you'll miss
c take the job
d How about
e you won't spend

8 A You are going to write a reply to Kenny in Ex 7A. Make a plan.

Paragraph 1: Options:
            Results:

Paragraph 2: Suggestions:
            Reasons:

B Write the reply. Use your notes in Ex 8A and the reply in Ex 7A to help you. Write 80–120 words.

Lesson 8C

HOW TO ... | check information
VOCABULARY | the environment
PRONUNCIATION | intonation in question tags

VOCABULARY

the environment

1 A Choose the correct word or phrase to complete the sentences.

1 I've become a .... because I don't want to eat meat.
   a vegetarian   **b** vet   **c** vehicle
2 Don't .... that bag away, I need it!
   a recycle   **b** improve   **c** throw
3 .... prices are increasing every day.
   a Energy   **b** Environment   **c** Pollution
4 We should .... all these old newspapers.
   a get smaller   **b** recycle   **c** throw
5 Can you turn the .... down?
   a heating   **b** pollution   **c** environment
6 We throw away a lot of .... each week.
   a pollution   **b** energy   **c** rubbish

B Complete the text with the words in the box.

> energy environment heating pollution
> recycling rubbish throw them away vegetarians

A different way of thinking

It's not always easy to think of ways to solve problems, but sometimes it can help if you think in a different way. Think of ways to make the problem worse, not better. So, for example, think about how to increase air and water ¹................ , not stop it.

We can buy new clothes every day, wear them once or twice and then ²................ . We can stop ³................ things so that we use paper, plastic, etc. only once. Then, we can put all this ⁴................ into the sea. We can have our ⁵................ on really high in all buildings in winter, even if people aren't living in them. That will use a lot of ⁶................ . We can also ask ⁷................ to start eating meat. That will increase the number of farm animals we need, the number of trees we cut down to make farms and the amount of carbon in the air.

Now let's take those ideas and do the OPPOSITE. They will help us to take better care of our ⁸................ .

How to ...

check information

2 A 🔊 **8.07** | Listen to a conversation. Complete the summary with one word in each gap.

The man is a ¹................ . The woman has become a ²................ but she's finding it hard. The man suggests that the woman eats some ³................ every week, but not every ⁴................ .

B 🔊 **8.07** | Choose the correct words to complete the sentences. Then listen and check.

1 You're a vegetarian, **are** / **aren't** you?
2 You're not a vegetarian, **are** / **aren't** you?
3 It's hard, **isn't** / **wasn't** it?
4 You're not saying 'stop being a vegetarian', **are** / **do** you?
5 You need to try something different, **do** / **don't** you?
6 And then you won't miss it, **will** / **won't** you?

PRONUNCIATION

3 🔊 **8.08** | intonation in question tags | Listen. Is the speaker sure (S) or not sure (N) of the answer?

1 ....   2 ....   3 ....   4 ....   5 ....   6 ....

SPEAKING

4 A 🔊 **8.09** | Complete the conversation with the words in the box and a pronoun (e.g. *it*). Listen and check.

> aren't can't did don't (x2) won't

A: We need to use less energy, ¹................ ?
B: Yes, energy prices are going up, ²................ ?
A: So, what shall we do?
B: We can turn down our heating by one degree. That'll help, ³................ ?
A: And we can remember to turn lights off.
B: Yes, and you can spend less time in the shower. You didn't need to spend ten minutes in there this morning, ⁴................ ?
A: No, I guess not. I love a hot shower though!
B: Me, too. People talk about a four-minute shower, ⁵................ ?
A: Four minutes! How is that enough time?
B: Well, you can turn off the water when you put shampoo in your hair.
A: But it'll be cold, ⁷................ ?
B: True, but you'll live!

B 🔊 **8.10** | You are B in in Ex 4A. Listen and speak after the beep. Record the conversation if you can.

C Listen to your recording and compare it to Ex 4A.

Speak anywhere Go to the interactive speaking practice

Lesson 8D

GRAMMAR | word building: nouns to adjectives
READING | the future of restaurants

GRAMMAR

word building: nouns to adjectives

1 A Choose the correct word or phrase to complete the sentences.

1 This area is very _____.
   a hilly   **b** hills   **c** hillier
2 Your shirt is very _____.
   a colours   **b** colourful   **c** colouring
3 Why is the air so _____?
   a smoked   **b** smokier   **c** smoky
4 It's _____ today than yesterday.
   a stormy   **b** stormier   **c** stormiest
5 This place is so quiet and _____.
   a peace   **b** peacely   **c** peaceful
6 Walk _____ across the road when the light is green.
   a careful   **b** carefuly   **c** carefully

B Complete the sentences with the correct form of the word in brackets.

1 I think it'll be nice and _____ (sun) later.
2 We love your painting. It's _____ (wonder)!
3 We were very _____ (luck) to win the match.
4 These biscuits are very _____ (taste).
5 Actions are more _____ (power) than words.
6 I'm so _____ (sleep) now. I need to go to bed.
7 I like sport but I don't think I'm _____ (sport).
8 It's wet and _____ (rain) today.

READING

2 A Read the article about restaurants in the future. Which topics (1–8) does it mention?

1 prices of meals
2 technology
3 restaurant staff
4 food recycling
5 size of restaurants
6 information on menus
7 cost of energy
8 restaurant meals

B Are the statements True (T) or False (F)?

1 Ryan is sure about his predictions for restaurants.
2 He says that in future everyone will use their phones to order food.
3 Restaurant staff will need to learn new things.
4 Ryan thinks that people will prefer to eat at a restaurant than at home.
5 He says that in the future, we'll choose a meal for health reasons.
6 Ryan thinks that restaurants will offer more food from around the world.
7 He says the fruit of the 'false banana' plant can make a tasty meal.
8 Ryan suggests we'll eat more insects in the future.

The future of restaurants

What will restaurants be like in twenty years' time? Ryan Whitely makes some predictions.

Imagine walking into a restaurant of the future. What do you see? Robots taking your order and serving you food? A menu with only food pills to try? Or maybe there'll be no restaurants at all?

It's hard to know exactly what a restaurant in 2050 will be like, but we can try and make some guesses. Firstly, technology will be important. Customers will arrive, use their phone to see the menu and then use the phone to order and pay for the food. In some places, that's already what happens. In restaurant kitchens, computer technology will cook the food and keep the kitchen clean. This means restaurants won't need so many staff and the staff they have will need new skills – technology skills.

In the future, it's possible that restaurants will be smaller, because more people will prefer to eat takeaway food at home. So, all restaurants will offer both food to eat in and food to take out. The menus might look a little different. These days, you can often find information about the meals on the menu, e.g. Is the meal vegetarian? How many calories are in the meal? In the future, there might be more information about what's in the meals and which meal is best for us. This is because we'll all have technology to tell us what our bodies need. We'll then choose a meal to match that.

The menu will probably have 'green' information, too. What effect does the meal have on the environment? Restaurants will probably sell more local food because it's better for the environment. We won't be able to buy food from the other side of the world. This might mean less choice.

Our changing weather will change the menus, too. Some things will become more difficult to grow, which means we might be eating different things. Some parts of the world might see more of the 'false banana' in meals – a plant similar to a banana plant that can create a delicious, high-calorie meal. Not with its fruit, which you can't eat, but with the rest of the plant along with other ingredients. We might also see a lot more insect dishes on the menu, too, and a lot more bean, nut and seaweed dishes.

So, we'll still eat out in restaurants and cafés in 2050, but the experience might be a little different to the experience today. I'm looking forward to seeing if my predictions come true!

7-8 REVIEW

GRAMMAR

1 Complete the sentences with words from Freya's calendar. Use verbs in the present continuous form.

> **Monday 3rd**
> Have lunch with Sarah 12 p.m. @ The Bistro
> See the dentist 2.30 p.m.
>
> **Tuesday 4th**
> Go for coffee with mum 10 a.m. Café Italia
> Take the train to York 16.14
>
> **Wednesday 5th**
> Go shopping with Kayley 11 a.m. Meet outside Brown's.
> Have meal out with Jason 8 p.m. Meet at my hotel at 7.45.
>
> **Thursday 6th**
> Have breakfast at hotel 7 a.m.
> Take train home 8.34 a.m.

1 On Monday, Freya .... with Sarah at 12.
2 She .... at 2.30.
3 At 10 on Tuesday, Freya and her mum .... at Café Italia.
4 She .... to York at 16.14.
5 On Wednesday, she .... with Kayley at 11.
6 Freya and Jason .... at 8. They .... at Freya's hotel.
7 On Thursday, she .... at her hotel at 7.
8 She .... home at 8.34.

2 The sentences below have a mistake. Choose the best option to correct the mistake.

1 Do you know <u>one people</u> that can fix my laptop?
 a anyone   b everyone   c no one
2 Everyone <u>wanting</u> coffee, not tea.
 a is want   b want   c wants
3 There's <u>zero</u> interesting to do or see around here.
 a nobody   b nothing   c nowhere
4 We're looking for somewhere nice <u>live</u>.
 a living   b to living   c to live

3 Put the words in the correct order to make sentences.

1 in the / a car / is there / middle / road? / of the / Why
2 left-hand / My house / of the street. / on the / is / side
3 strange animal / in the / a / There's / distance.
4 back / photo? / Who's / at the / of the / that woman
5 back / cinema. / Let's / at the / sit / of the
6 the girl / hair. / long red / Felicity's / with the
7 only person / without / I'm the / in the picture / a hat.
8 you / a lovely old / waiting for / I'm / in front / building. / of

4 Read the answer to the question. Complete the sentences with the correct form of *will* and the words in brackets.

> **What** [1] .... **(life / be) like in 2050?**
>
> **@PaulH**
> Well, let's think about life thirty years ago. There weren't any smartphones and social media wasn't popular, so yes, I think 2050 [2] .... (probably / be) different. Technology will be different. We [3] .... (not / have) the same kinds of phones as today. I'm sure we [4] .... (not / use) the internet exactly the same as we do now. We [5] .... (probably / drive) different types of cars. However, I don't think that [6] .... (everything / change). Many things will stay the same. I [7] .... (be / sure / we / spend) time with our friends and families just like we do now and just like people did thirty years ago. We'll work. We'll eat. We'll do sport and have hobbies. [8] .... (life in 2050 / be) different to life today? Yes. [9] .... (maybe / we / work) different hours, eat different food and do different activities, but our daily lives [10] .... (be) similar in many ways, too.

5 Choose the correct verbs to complete the sentences.

1 If you **take** / **will take** the job, you **don't** / **won't** work so many hours.
2 Ren **asks** / **will ask** you for help if she **needs** / **will need** it.
3 **Do you watch** / **Will you watch** that video if you **have** / **will have** time later?
4 If we **leave** / **will leave** now, we **get** / **'ll get** there on time.
5 If we **don't leave** / **will** leave now, we **'ll** / **won't** be late.
6 You **don't** / **won't** pass your test if you **don't study** / **study**.
7 If it **snow** / **snows** tomorrow, I **'ll** / **won't** go to work.
8 William **sleeps** / **will sleep** here if he **misses** / **will miss** the last train home.

6 Complete the adjectives with the correct letters.

1 This drink is too sugar............ for me.
2 I've got a really pain............ stomach ache.
3 No one in my family is very sport............
4 Thank you for everything. You've been very help............
5 I started a business which is quite success............ now.
6 It's very wind............ and rain............ outside today.
7 This thing here is very use............ in the kitchen.
8 Someone's made a fire outside. It's smok............ and smell............

58

REVIEW 7–8

VOCABULARY

7 Complete each phrase with a verb.
1 .... on a tour, shopping, sightseeing
2 .... an evening out, a night in, a rest
3 .... a show, some live music, a band
4 .... to a club, to the theatre, to a market
5 .... a race, a tennis match, TV

8 Complete the conversation with the words in the box. There are three words you do not need.

bottle   box   carton   containers   deliver   mug
order   pick   pots   takeaway   tip   tube   use

A: Shall we get a ¹............................? I don't want to cook.
B: OK, how about pizza? Or would you prefer some chicken?
A: Pizza, I think.
B: Fine. I'll ²............................ us a large margherita and two drinks.
A: There's a ³............................ of juice in the fridge and a ⁴............................ of water. Can we have those?
B: Fine. There are some ⁵............................ of yoghurt in the fridge and a ⁶............................ of chocolates in the cupboard, so we don't need dessert.
A: Will you ⁷............................ the app to order the food?
B: No, I'll call. I don't have the app on my phone.
A: Ask them what time they'll ⁸............................ the pizza.
B: Or shall I ⁹............................ it up? It might be faster.
A: No, we can wait. I just need time to find some money for the delivery rider. We should give them a ¹⁰............................

9 Choose the correct words to complete the sentences.
1 You **don't let / mustn't** touch the food.
2 The hotel doesn't **allow / let** children in the swimming pool.
3 You **can't / should** take drinks into the theatre. It's not OK.
4 My parents don't **allow / let** me stay out late.
5 They **'ve banned / mustn't** fireworks in the city.
6 You **can't / shouldn't** lean on the window. It's a bad idea.

10 Match the sentence beginnings (1–8) with the endings (a–h).
1 I'm sure chocolate bars are getting
2 Nothing ever stays
3 If you run every day, you'll get
4 The speed of
5 The price of milk is
6 My English is
7 The price of petrol has gone
8 It's becoming

a faster and faster.
b warmer outside.
c smaller every year!
d down by a few pence.
e delivery is quite fast.
f the same in life.
g increasing every week.
h improving all the time!

11 Complete the word in each sentence. The first letter is given.
1 Things go wrong, but you must always try to look on the b............................ side.
2 I h............................ that you have a great time at your grandparents.
3 It was very noisy last night. It was i............................ for me to sleep.
4 My d............................ is to be a top chef. I hope it comes true!
5 No one is successful all the time. Everyone f............................ sometimes.
6 I can only see the negative s............................ of the job, not the positive.

12 Complete the social media post with the words in the box.

energy   environment   heating   pollution
recycle   rubbish   throw   vegetarian

We all know that we need to do more for the ¹............................ because if we take too much from our planet, there'll be nothing left in the future. We know that we need to stop burning wood because it creates air ²............................. We know that we should reuse things until they break so we put less ³............................ in the ground. But if we have to ⁴............................ things away, we should try to ⁵............................ them so we can use the material again. We know that we should turn our ⁶............................ down in buildings in winter so we save ⁷............................. We also know we should become ⁸............................ or at least stop eating so much meat. The question is, why don't we do these things? Maybe it's because people don't want to believe that bad things will happen in the future and they prefer to look on the bright side. What are your thoughts?

59

1–4 CUMULATIVE REVIEW

GRAMMAR

questions

1 Complete the questions with one word.
1 .... you live near here?
2 Where .... Maisie today?
3 .... sort of food does Callum like?
4 .... of these books is your favourite?
5 .... far is the bank from here?
6 How .... suitcases are you bringing?

present simple and continuous

2 Choose the correct verbs to complete the message.

Hi Lizzie, I ¹**'m standing / stand** at the top of the Eiffel Tower at the moment! The view is amazing! I ²**'m spending / spend** two weeks in France this summer. I ³**'m thinking / think** of staying for longer and finding work here because it's such a great city. The food isn't cheap, and my hotel ⁴**is costing / costs** more than I can afford, but I ⁵**loving / love** it. It's in the oldest part of the city and it's beautiful. I ⁶**'m feeling / feel** very happy these days!

verb + -ing form

3 Find and correct one mistake in each sentence.
1 Sophie loves swim in the sea.
2 I really hate wakeing up early.
3 Sonny dislikes play team sports.
4 Most days, I don't mind to make dinner.
5 I love begining a new notebook.
6 We enjoy don't getting up early in the holidays.

all, some, both, none of them

4 Read the information about a family and complete the sentences with *all*, *most*, *some* or *none*.

My family
20/20 people live in Bainbridge.
15/20 people have a job in the car industry.
0/20 people play team sports.
9/20 people hate strawberries. Strange!
18/20 drive.
10/20 can play the piano, guitar or something else.

1 .... of us live in Bainbridge.
2 .... of us work in the car industry.
3 .... of us enjoy team sports.
4 .... of us can't stand strawberries.
5 .... of us drive a car.
6 .... of us play musical instruments.

have to, don't have to, can't

5 Complete each second sentence so that it means the same as the first. Use *have to*, *don't have to* or *can't*.
1 Please wear jackets in the restaurant.
   Visitors to the restaurant .... a jacket.
2 Museum visitors can leave their bags here but it is not necessary.
   Visitors to the museum .... their bags when they enter the building.
3 Do not wear shoes in the dance studio.
   Visitors .... shoes in the dance studio.
4 Towels are available for any gym users at no extra cost.
   Gym users .... pay to use the gym's towels.

present perfect simple (1)

6 Complete the conversations with the present perfect or past simple form of the verb in brackets or the correct short answer.

A: ¹ .... (you / ever / ride) a horse?
B: No, I ² .... Have you?
A: Yes, I ³ .... (ride) one when I was young.
B: How old ⁴ .... (be) you?
A: About thirteen.

A: Where's Hannah?
B: She ⁵ .... (go) to the supermarket. She's at the one on Baker Street. Do you know it?
A: No. I ⁶ .... (never / go) to that one.

A: I ⁷ .... (never / see) a film like this. It's just terrible!
B: I ⁸ .... (watch) a few terrible films in my life. This isn't the worse.
A: Wow. ⁹ .... (you / ever / leave) the cinema in the middle of a film?
B: Yes, I ¹⁰ .... Lots of times!
A: I ¹¹ .... , but I'm going to start now!

VOCABULARY

common verbs; everyday activities

7 Complete each phrase with the correct verb.
1 .... your hair after you wash it so it's not wet
2 .... to sleep for an hour in the afternoon
3 .... the washing up after dinner
4 .... a gym for £50 a month
5 .... the door with your key when you leave the house
6 .... dressed after you have a shower
7 .... for a bus to come
8 .... your clothes away in the cupboard

CUMULATIVE REVIEW 1–4

animals

8 Choose the correct words to complete the article.

Amazing animals

The magnificent frigatebird is a large seabird. It has brown-black ¹**feathers / shells**. It can fly up to 2,500 metres above sea level. Its ²**webs / wings** are over two metres long from end to end when open. The male bird has a kind of red bag on its front. It fills with air when the bird tries to find a female.

The velvet ant is a type of ³**insect / spider** like a bee or wasp. It makes a high sound when it's stressed. The male has ⁴**trunks / wings** and flies but the female doesn't. The female has long hair all over the ⁵**skin / tails** on its body.

The maned wolf isn't actually a wolf. It's more similar to a wild dog or ⁶**fox / spider**. It usually lives alone in parts of South America. It has red-brown ⁷**fur / shell**, long legs and big ears. It has a long ⁸**tail / trunk** which is white at the end.

actions

9 Complete the verbs. The first letter is given.

1 Would you like me to c_____ your suitcase to your room?
2 Can you a_____ the phone? I'm cooking.
3 I'd love someone to b_____ me a coffee in bed!
4 I'm afraid we have to c_____ our meeting tomorrow. I have another appointment.
5 Can you h_____ the door open for us, please?
6 Let's t_____ a break and get a drink.
7 I'm always busy, but I try to m_____ time for exercise each day.

knowing, understanding and thinking; school and university subjects

10 Complete the sentences with the words in the box.

| develop | discover | drama | expect |
| medicine | plan | politics | tourism |

1 People who become doctors study _____.
2 History students try to _____ new information about the past.
3 Students of _____ learn all about the travel industry.
4 Some business studies students _____ to start a new business in the future.
5 Students of economics _____ to learn about money.
6 _____ teachers have to explain different government systems.
7 _____ students might have experience of both the theatre and film.
8 IT students _____ new systems for computers.

location, position and movement

11 Choose the correct words to complete the sentences.

1 Wait for me **out of / outside**. I'll be there soon.
2 Stand **beside / together** me for this photo.
3 That painting is **up and down / upside-down**.
4 Go straight on, **above / over** the bridge.
5 Move **around / forwards** a few steps. Then you can see the view better.
6 Shall I take the shopping **onto / out of** the bags?

travel; travel phrases

12 Complete the conversation with the words in the box.

| border | coast | distance | journey |
| routes | travel | trip | way |

I've got the day off! I'm on a day ¹_____.
I'm on my ²_____ to Sidmouth.

Is that on the ³_____ of England and Wales?

No. Sidmouth is on the south ⁴_____.

How's the ⁵_____?

The ⁶_____ isn't long, but the traffic is terrible. We've tried two different ⁷_____. Both are bad.

Summer traffic is awful! I always prefer train ⁸_____!

How to …

13 Complete the words in the conversations.

encourage people

A: I'm worried about the wedding.
B: That's all ¹r_____. It's natural to be worried.
A: I have to speak in front of lots of people.
B: I ²u_____. But I think you'll ³b_____ great!

make and accept offers

A: Is that someone at the door? ⁴S_____ I get it?
B: I ⁵c_____ get it. I think it's Jan.
A: But you're really busy. ⁶L_____ me do it.
B: OK. That would be a great ⁷h_____, thanks.

give instructions and check understanding

A: ⁸F_____, open the paint carefully.
B: ⁹L_____ this?
A: Yes, that's right. You should ¹⁰a_____ wear gloves so you don't get paint everywhere.
B: OK. What do I need to do ¹¹n_____?

make suggestions and recommendations

A: Where ¹²c_____ we get some coffee?
B: Why ¹³d_____ we go to that new café?
A: Good idea. How ¹⁴a_____ having lunch too?
B: That's ¹⁵f_____ with me.

61

5–8 CUMULATIVE REVIEW

GRAMMAR

quantifiers

1 Choose the word or phrase which does NOT fit the sentence.
1 I don't have **a lot of / much / no** free time.
2 I've got **a bit of / too many / too much** work to do today.
3 Sandy hasn't got **lots of / enough / a little** friends in the area.
4 Would you like **any / some / too much** juice?
5 I'm going to make **a / some / many** coffee.
6 It's **too / too much / very** hot in this room.
7 Do you want **a bit of / a little / not enough** chocolate?
8 We've got **any / some / no** cheese.

adverbs of frequency and manner

2 Find and correct one mistake in each sentence.
1 I always am in the office on Fridays.
2 They come occasionally to stay with us.
3 Never, Liam and I see each other these days.
4 We go out normally for a walk in the mornings.
5 Why are you running so fastly?
6 I think I can cook good than you.
7 You sing really good.
8 Something smells strangely in here.

present perfect simple (2)

3 Use the prompts to complete the conversation.

Morning! ¹_____ (you / have got / Mum / a birthday present / yet)?

No, not yet.

Me neither. I ²_____ (still / not / got) any idea what to get her.

I ³_____ (already / decide) to get her theatre tickets.

Good idea!

But I ⁴_____ (not / have / time / to look for any tickets / yet)

Oh! I ⁵_____ (just / have) a thought. Can we give her a night out together?

Sure! I'll pay for the tickets and you can pay for dinner.

present continuous with future reference; other future forms

4 Choose the correct words to complete the post. More than one answer might be possible.

I've got a really fun day today. I ¹**'m meeting / meeting / meet** Michal at 10 a.m at the train station. We ²**'go / 're going / 're going to go** into the city. We ³**'re going to take / 're taking / take** the 10.22 train so we arrive at lunchtime because we ⁴**eating / eat / 're going to eat** out at a great restaurant I read about. I don't know what I'll do after lunch. Michal ⁵**'s going / 's going to / go** to a work meeting. I expect that I ⁶**'ll walk / walk / 'm walking** around for a bit. Then, tonight, we ⁷**see / seeing / 're seeing** a basketball match. A friend from university ⁸**is coming / comes / 's going to come** too. I can't wait!

adverbial and prepositional phrases

5 Add one word to each sentence.
1 Is Mariana the girl long dark hair?
2 Use the glass the right-hand side of you.
3 I thought I saw a plane in distance, but it was just a bird!
4 Eric loves lying in the middle his garden with a book.
5 We usually park our car in front our house.
6 I usually sit in the chair the back of the class.

first conditional

6 Choose the correct verbs to complete the reply to the question.

Should I get a second job?

The main reason for getting a second job is money. If you ¹**have / will have** a second job, you'll have more money each month. For some people, a second job is necessary. If they ²**don't have / will not have** two jobs, they won't have enough money to pay their rent, food, etc. at the start of the month. If you have some extra cash at the end of next month, you ³**increase / will increase** your savings.

A second reason to get a second job is experience. You ⁴**learn / 'll learn** new skills if you do something different to your main job. If you ⁵**decide / will decide** you love it, you ⁶**have / 'll have** the chance to make it your main job.

It's hard to suggest a job without knowing much about you. If you ⁷**love / 'll love** nature, you ⁸**enjoy / 'll enjoy** taking people's dogs for a walk. If you ⁹**like / will like** making things, you ¹⁰**be / will be** happy to make and sell them online. If you ¹¹**like / will like** social media, you ¹²**probably love / 'll probably love** making videos and sharing them. Think about what you enjoy and are good at.

CUMULATIVE REVIEW 5–8

VOCABULARY

money and value

7 Complete the sentences with the words in the box.

> cost   offers   rent   savings   spend   valuable

1 I love this clock. It's not .... but I've had it a long time.
2 How much did your coat .... ?
3 I've just spent all my .... on a new laptop.
4 Here's £20. Don't .... it all on sweets!
5 I want to .... an electric bike for a day.
6 We've had two .... to buy our house!

sports collocations

8 Choose the two sports in each group that do NOT go with the verb.

1 go: **baseball / bowling / hockey / scuba diving / snowboarding / windsurfing**
2 play: **badminton / cricket / rugby / sailing / snooker / table tennis / t'ai chi**
3 do: **athletics / exercise / judo / karate / skiing / volleyball / yoga**

health and illness; the body and symptoms

9 Choose the correct words to complete the social media posts.

> **What are some silly ways you've hurt yourself?**
>
> **Anabella**
> Most people fall down stairs. I fell up them! I really hurt the big ¹**finger / toe** on my right foot, so I went to see my doctor at his ²**office / surgery**. He did some tests and the ³**results / treatment** showed that it was broken. There was no helpful ⁴**symptom / treatment** and the doctor gave me no ⁵**emergency / prescription** for medicine. I just had to take ⁶**painkillers / virus** and rest my foot.
>
> **Keith**
> I fell asleep on the train. When I woke up, my head was on my neighbour's ⁷**ankle / shoulder** (I didn't know him!) and I had a terrible stiff ⁸**neck / throat**. It hurt a lot!

going out and staying in

10 Complete the sentences with a verb in the correct form.

1 Shall we go out tonight or .... a night in?
2 Let's .... the basketball game on TV.
3 I .... out with some friends last night.
4 Jamie has never .... a play at the theatre.
5 There's a TV at the sports café. We can sit and .... the race there.
6 Let's leave the house and .... for a coffee.

attitudes

11 Complete the conversations with the words in the box.

> bright   dream   experience   failed
> hope   impossible   negative   worry

Last week
A: I've got a job interview tomorrow. It's for a chef.
B: Great! I ¹................................ they'll see how much you love food and cooking.
A: Me too! My ²................................ is to open my own restaurant one day.

Today
A: I didn't get the job. They asked me to make a dish in fifteen minutes. It was ³................................ to make something good in such a short time. My dish was bad. I ⁴................................ !
B: Oh dear. Still, look on the ⁵................................ side. You can plan things to cook before your next interview.
A: I can only see the ⁶................................ side at the moment but you're right. I can learn from the ⁷................................. But I ⁸................................ I won't have the chance again.

the environment

12 Complete the words for the definitions.

1 the natural things around us: trees, plants, etc.: e................................
2 use materials again: r................................
3 the things we throw away: r................................
4 dirty air, water, etc.: p................................
5 a person who doesn't eat meat: v................................

How to …

talk about a product

13 Choose the correct words to complete the text.

> We ¹**all / most** want to do exercise, but lots of us have busy lives and don't have time. Well, here's the ²**answer / problem**. It's the desk bike. It's an exercise bike you can sit on at your desk. It's ³**got / has** information about your speed, distance and time. ⁴**Also / Another** good thing about the desk bike is that you can exercise your arms. But perhaps the ⁵**best / better** thing is that you can put it under your desk. Why is this ⁶**important / perfect**? Because it keeps your office tidy. I ⁷**really / very** love my desk bike and you're going to love ⁸**your / yours**, too!

ask for and give permission

14 Put the words in the correct order to make sentences.

1 this table? / for us / to use / all right / Is it
2 a minute? / borrow / for / your phone / Could I
3 to help yourself / feel / to food. / Please / free
4 not / afraid / possible. / I'm / that's
5 could use / think / your toilet? / I / Do you
6 loudly / mustn't / in here. / You / talk

1–8 CUMULATIVE REVIEW

GRAMMAR

past simple and continuous

1 Complete the sentences with the past simple or past continuous form of the verbs in brackets.

1. I .... (stand) in the street when a fox .... (run) past!
2. You .... (not / help) while I .... (cook).
3. Alana .... (get up) early yesterday while everyone .... (sleep).
4. I .... (not / do) a lot of work while I .... (study) at university.
5. We .... (learn) English in Dublin when we .... (meet).
6. While Alex .... (not / look), I .... (take) his last piece of pizza!

definite article: *the*

2 Complete the advertisements with *the* or no article (–).

Wanted before [1] .... 30th March

Dining room table and four chairs. [2] .... table must be large and round. We can pick it up after six in [3] .... evening.

FOR SALE

Almost new desk exercise bike. [4] .... bike sits under your desk so you can exercise at work. Collect from [5] .... Bridgeton, near [6] .... Adley Station, at any time. £20.

3 Complete the sentences with *had/have to*, *didn't have to* or *couldn't*.

1. You .... give me a gift but I'm happy you did!
2. We .... stay in the library after five. It closed.
3. Arlo .... to go to work really early this morning. He left at five.
4. Did you .... do sport at school today?
5. Kazue .... help, but she wanted to.
6. I was late. I .... say sorry to the teacher.

subject and object questions

4 Choose the correct words to complete the questions.

1. A: What time **does the film start / starts the film**?
   B: At 9 p.m. I think.
2. A: What **do you make / makes** you angry?
   B: Rude people. It's not hard to be nice to people!
3. A: Who **does / do you do** the housework?
   B: We all share the work.
4. A: Who **did bring / brought** the cake?
   B: Maggie. It's her birthday today.
5. A: When **did you arrive / arrived you**?
   B: I got here about an hour ago.
6. A: Who **ate / did you eat** the rest of the chicken?
   B: Me. I ate it for lunch.

comparatives and superlatives

5 Complete the article with the comparative or superlative form of the adjectives in brackets. Add other words where necessary.

Three fantastic learning holidays

A learning holiday can be a lot [1] .... (interesting) than a beach holiday. You learn more about the country, meet more people and go home with a new skill. Here are three learning holidays you could try.

Salsa dancing in Cuba

Cuba is one of [2] .... (colourful) places in the world and salsa is one of [3] .... (popular) dances. You'll take lessons and have nights out dancing at local clubs.

Cooking in Thailand

Thai dishes are some of [4] .... (tasty) meals in the world. You'll go to markets, learn to cook amazing dishes and go home with [5] .... (good) cooking skills than when you arrived.

Painting in Morocco

The buildings in Morocco are some of [6] .... (lovely) in the world. They can also be some of [7] .... (difficult) to paint. But with help from amazing painters, you'll develop the skills you need to paint them. If you're a beginner, then try painting in Spain. The buildings are beautiful but a little [8] .... (easy) to paint than in Morocco.

verbs of sensation + adjective or *like*

6 Complete the facts with the correct form of the words in brackets.

OUR SENSES   Did you know?

1. Everyone .... (smell / different). No two people smell the same!
2. Spicy food .... (feel / hot) in our mouths but it's not. Our brain just thinks it is.
3. Food .... (only / taste / good) when we can smell it.
4. Sweet food .... (taste / delicious) because our brain knows it gives us energy.
5. Food items sometimes .... (taste / bad) so we don't eat them because they might make us ill.
6. If something .... (smell / good), it can make you happier.

64

CUMULATIVE REVIEW 1–8

possessive pronouns, whose, this/that, there/then

7 Complete the sentences with one word in each gap.
1 We both have cars. I like mine, but _____ is nicer.
2 What's _____ note here? Is it for me?
3 _____ car shall we take?
4 Is this Jenna's bag? She was sitting here, but I don't think it's _____.
5 Your grandparents live around here, don't they? Is that house _____?
6 That dog is trying to catch _____ tail!

verbs with two objects

8 Choose the correct phrases to complete the conversation. Sometimes both are possible.

A: Don't eat all the bread, please. Leave some ¹**me / for me**!
B: Is that all we've got? I offered ²**more to buy / to buy more**, but you said we didn't need it.
A: We didn't this morning, but then Callum made ³**some sandwiches for his friends / to his friends some sandwiches**.
B: OK. I'll buy ⁴**us / for us** some more later.
A: Thanks. Did you send ⁵**flowers to your mum / your mum flowers** for her birthday?
B: Yes, and I wrote ⁶**her a card / a card for her**, too.
A: That's nice. I'll send ⁷**her a message / for her a message** in the morning.

be + adjective + to infinitive

9 Match the sentence beginnings (1–6) with the endings (a–f).
1 It's usual for me to
2 It's hard for
3 It's really kind
4 I was sorry
5 Be careful
6 It's better to

a me to talk about my feelings.
b have too many friends than not enough.
c not to forget your keys.
d of you to come and visit us.
e have a big lunch each day.
f to hear about Jonny.

indefinite pronouns: someone, nothing, anywhere, etc.

10 Complete the conversation with indefinite pronouns.

A: There's an emergency and I'm dealing with it all on my own. Isn't there ¹_____ who can help me?
B: ²_____ is busy at the moment except Ken.
A: I just need ³_____ to help me move things out of the office cupboard. There's water ⁴_____ – it's all over the floor. I don't want ⁵_____ on the shelves to get wet.
B: Then, ask Ken. His desk is ⁶_____ on the second floor.
A: Brilliant, thanks! There's ⁷_____ heavy, but it might take some time to move it all.

will for predictions

11 Complete the conversation with 'll or won't and the prompts in brackets.

A: It's our first big night out this year!
B: Let me predict what ¹_____ (happen). Harry ²_____ (have) an argument with Vanessa. They ³_____ (not / talk) to each other for the rest of the night. But I ⁴_____ (sure / they / be) best friends again tomorrow. They always are.
A: Who ⁵_____ (lose) their mobile phone? There's always someone.
B: It ⁶_____ (probably / be) me. It was last time!

word building: nouns to adjectives

12 Correct the form of one word in each sentence.
1 This curry is too spice for me.
2 You look wonder today.
3 It's not flat where I live – it's hill.
4 It's too noise to work in here.
5 We need to be care not to wake the baby.
6 Thank you, you've been very help.

How to ...

check information

13 Complete the questions with the correct words.
1 You weren't born in the city, _____?
2 It's not cold outside, _____?
3 The lesson was fun yesterday, _____?
4 You won't forget to call me, _____?
5 You've seen this film before, _____?
6 You and Rachel can take a taxi home, _____?

14 Use the prompts to complete the conversations.

make and accept offers

A: ¹_____ you a sandwich? (shall / make)
B: ²_____ great, thanks. (that / be)

A: This recipe is hard to understand
B: ³_____ you. (let / help)
A: Thanks. That's ⁴_____. (kind / you)

A: Do ⁵_____ that bag? (want / me / carry)
B: Thanks, but ⁶_____ (I / OK).

talk about health problems

A: What can I do for you?
B: I ⁷_____ (worried / my wrist). I think I ⁸_____ (break / it).

A: How can I help you?
B: My ⁹_____ (whole body / aches).
A: When ¹⁰_____ (these symptoms / start)?
B: Yesterday.
A: It ¹¹_____ (sound / like) you've got a virus. You ¹²_____ (should / stay / home) and rest.

1–8 CUMULATIVE REVIEW

VOCABULARY

job phrases; jobs

1 Choose the correct words to complete the texts.

> I worked in the furniture ¹**career / industry** for five years. It was my ²**job / work** to deliver furniture to people's homes. I liked my colleagues and the customers, but the furniture was heavy and it gave me terrible backache. Someone ³**offered / signed** me a job as a flower delivery driver and I took it. Much less painful!

> I was the ⁴**personal assistant / dentist** for the owner of a fashion magazine, so I did everything for her. She was lovely when I had my interview and I was excited to ⁵**develop / sign** the contract. The ⁶**pay / savings** was amazing, but nothing I did was right. I left after a year and completely changed my ⁷**career / industry** to become a fashion writer. Then I ⁸**developed / offered** my own writing business.

feelings

2 Complete the adjective for each definition. The first letter is given.

1. happy: p...................
2. worried something bad will happen: a...................
3. unhappy because you're alone: l...................
4. feeling good about the future: p...................
5. worried and tired: s...................
6. sure of your ability: c...................

air travel; at the airport

3 Complete the conversation with the words and phrases in the box.

> board   boarding pass   check-in desk
> delay   departure lounge   flight
> passport control   security

A: I've lost my ¹...................
B: Where did you have it last?
A: I got it at the ²................... and then I had it when we went through ³....................
B: And what about when we went through ⁴...................? Did you take it out of your bag?
A: Yes, because someone looked at it. Then I bought something in the ⁵................... and I had to show it to the shop assistant.
B: So, it's between the shop and here. You can't ⁶................... the plane without it!
A: I know! What time does our ⁷................... leave?
B: Soon! But I think there's a fifteen-minute ⁸................... so there's still time!

positive adjectives

4 Complete the adjectives that describe the people or things. The first letter is given.

1. Tom knows a lot about everything. He's very c....................
2. Lots of people like chocolate ice cream. It's very p....................
3. Both players are very good. Their skills are e....................
4. The story isn't a lie. It's r....................
5. I loved the cake. It was d....................

irregular past participles

5 Write the correct past participle form of the verbs.

1. buy   ....
2. ride   ....
3. read   ....
4. win   ....
5. teach ....
6. write ....

giving gifts

6 Complete the advertisement with the words in the box.

> get   presents   prices   receive   special   unusual

> If you need to ¹................... a gift for a loved one, click here. You'll find amazing gifts at both low and high ².................... There are funny ³..................., like silly mugs and T-shirts. There are extra ⁴................... presents, like rings and watches. And there are ⁵................... gifts that people don't normally give, like afternoon tea at a five-star hotel or a drive in a racing car. Whatever you choose, your loved one will be happy to ⁶................... a gift from our website.

countable and uncountable nouns

7 Put the nouns into the correct column in the table.

> bag   carrot   electricity   fashion
> furniture   luggage   meal   message
> minute   music   tip   work

countable nouns	uncountable nouns

66

CUMULATIVE REVIEW 1–8

common adjectives

8 Choose the correct words to complete the phrases. More than one answer might be possible.
1. a **thick / thin / weak** coat
2. **dark / light / soft** blue
3. a **full / metal / plastic** clock
4. a **narrow / thick / wide** street
5. **light / strong / weak** arms
6. a **full / plastic / soft** toy
7. a **dark / empty / heavy** room
8. a/an **empty / full / weak** bowl

actions; physical actions

9 Complete the notices with the words in the box.

> down   forget   get   have   left   push   take

1. When you .... the door open, be careful of people on the other side.
2. If you .... an accident at work, please call the HR department on 1122.
3. Please don't .... somebody else's lunch from the fridge.
4. If you have .... something in a meeting room, please go and tell someone at Reception.
5. Please don't try to .... things .... from the top shelf yourself. Call 3598 for help.
6. Don't .... to email bookings@clm.mail.uk if you need to book an online meeting room.

eating out and eating in; containers

10 Match the sentence beginnings (1–6) with the endings (a–f).
1. Have we got a new tube
2. Let's order food from a delivery
3. Shall I make a pot
4. I'd love a packet
5. Have we got a jar
6. I can go and pick

a. of tea or coffee?
b. of honey?
c. of toothpaste?
d. up a takeaway.
e. of crisps.
f. meal service.

permission

11 Complete the email with the phrases (a–e).

Hi Ann,

I just got an email from the museum with some important information about the school visit there.

1. They .... mobile phones during school visits.
2. They .... children to take large bags into the museum.
3. They .... anyone eat or drink in the museum, except at the museum café.
4. The children .... any work of art at the museum.
5. They .... against the walls of the museum. The walls are white and get dirty easily.

Please give the children in your class this information. Thanks!

Shawna

a. shouldn't lean
b. don't let
c. 've banned
d. don't allow
e. mustn't touch

change

12 Complete the social media post with the words and phrases in the box.

> become   down   get faster
> improve   speed   the same

Do you think humans will continue to develop in the future? Will we ¹............ and see a person run 100 metres under nine seconds? Will we ²............ cleverer and really understand the meaning of life? Will we ³............ our skills in medicine and live to be 150? Or will the ⁴............ of change slow down and the number of new things we discover about the human body go ⁵............ each year to almost nothing? In this situation, our human skills and abilities will stay about ⁶............ as they are now. What are your thoughts?

AUDIOSCRIPTS

UNIT 1

Audio 1.01
1 Who's your closest friend?
2 What colour are his eyes?
3 Does Ben live on his own?
4 Do you like chocolate cake?
5 How can I help you?
6 Do you ever play volleyball?

Audio 1.02
1 What are you doing today?
2 Why are you sitting in here?
3 Who are they talking about?
4 What are we waiting for?
5 Where are they living now?

Audio 1.03
People pay a Japanese man called Shoji Morimoto to go out with them, because they don't want to go alone. It could be to a restaurant, a party or a wedding. One person even paid him to say goodbye to them at a train station when they left Tokyo to move to a different city.

Audioscript 1.04
Presenter: On Monday, we talked about Shoji Morimoto and his unusual job. Well, today I'm talking to someone else with an unusual job. This is Marta Morales. She gets paid to go to weddings, but she doesn't plan the wedding. Marta, what do you do at them?
Marta: Brides pay me around £2,000 to be their friend on their special day.
Presenter: Why?
Marta: There are many different reasons. Sometimes the bride doesn't have any friends. Sometimes the bride has a lot of friends, but they're all very quiet and she needs someone who's a bit more exciting. And sometimes it's because the bride's friends don't like each other.
Presenter: Right. So, what's your job when they don't like each other?
Marta: My job is to stop people from arguing and to make sure everyone is happy.
Presenter: Do the wedding guests know that the bride is paying you?
Marta: Every wedding is different. At some weddings, everyone knows that I'm doing a job. At other weddings, they think I'm a friend or maybe a cousin.
Presenter: What happens before the wedding? Do you make a plan with the bride?
Marta: Yes. I meet the bride a few weeks before the wedding and we decide together what my story is. I'm preparing for a wedding at the moment. We've decided to tell everyone that I'm the bride's cousin from a city far away!
Presenter: So, when did you begin this unusual career?
Marta: It was five years ago, after I went to a lot of my friend's weddings and learnt that I was good at helping everything to go well.
Presenter: What did you do before that?
Marta: I had a very different job! I worked in a shop, but I was a bit bored, so I decided to start my own company. I couldn't believe how many brides wanted my help!
Presenter: Do you enjoy your job?
Marta: Most of the time, I feel very happy with what I do. Weddings are very special, but my job is to make sure everyone is having a good time and that can be difficult. I usually get home feeling very tired!

Audio 1.05
1 It's fine, really.
2 You can do it!
3 It looks great!
4 That's all right.
5 What do you think?
6 I know what you mean.

Audio 1.06
1
A: What are you doing?
B: I'm painting my kitchen. Look! What do you think?
A: Wow! It looks great! Nice colour.
B: Thanks! I only started it a few hours ago, but I've nearly finished it.
A: Well done! It's not an easy room to paint.

2
A: Oh, I'm so tired. I don't think I can finish.
B: You're nearly there. Just a few more minutes. You can do it!
A: I can't.
B: You can! Go on! Keep running!
A: OK! I can try.

3
A: I'm so sorry. The bus was late and then it stopped at the wrong place.
B: That's all right. I thought it was probably a bus problem.
A: But I missed the meeting. I really wanted to be there. I was so pleased when you invited me. Next time, I'll get an earlier bus and …
B: Don't worry. It's fine really. Just get a coffee and relax. You look very stressed!

4
A: We have to give a presentation to the class on Friday.
B: Yes.
A: But I'm not very confident.
B: Not everyone likes giving presentations. I understand.
A: Can I give the presentation with another student?
B: That's a great idea! Yes, that's fine.

Audio 1.07 and 1.08
A: My cousin wants me to introduce her and her new husband at their wedding dinner, but I've never talked in front of a lot of people before.
B: I know what you mean. It's scary.
A: And my brother doesn't think I can do it.
B: Oh no! It's not important what he thinks. What do you think?
A: I think I can do it.
B: Then don't worry. Give the introduction.
A: Can I practise with you now?
B: Yes, that's a good idea!
A: OK, here goes … Ladies and Gentlemen, your attention, please. Please stand for the bride and groom, Mr and Mrs Brooks!
B: Oh, well done! That was great! Very clear and confident.
A: Thanks! So, shall I tell my cousin I can do it?
B: Yes, you'll be great!

Audio 1.09
A: Millie, do you want to meet up and do something tomorrow?
B: Yes, that'd be great, Louis. Let's go for a walk.
A: I hate walking.
B: What? How can you hate walking?
A: It's slow and boring. And it's really cold outside at the moment. I prefer to stay inside in the warm.

AUDIOSCRIPTS

B: I love walking! I can get some exercise and look at the trees. And when it's cold, I can stop at a little café and get a hot chocolate. Wonderful!
A: I don't like hot chocolate.
B: What?! I didn't know this about you. What else do you dislike?
A: I don't like getting up for work on Mondays.
B: Well, that's normal. I don't like Sunday evenings, because I start thinking about work.
A: I love playing games, but I hate losing.
B: Oh, I knew that. You always want to win. I like winning, but I don't mind losing. It's just fun to play.
A: I don't like waking up late during the week. I like to get to work early so I don't need to stay in the office late and I can leave on time.
B: I know what you mean, but waking up late at the weekend is worse. I want to use every minute of my weekend for fun. What else don't you like?
A: Er … I don't like having baths. I prefer to have a shower.
B: Really? I don't like having baths in the summer, but in the winter, I love them. I can stay in the bath for ages!
A: I imagine that you like swimming.
B: I love it! I don't go to the swimming pool here very often, but I love swimming in hotel pools when I'm on holiday. I'd love to have my own pool.
A: I'd like that too, but I hate swimming in public swimming pools. They're always too cold.
B: You really don't like the cold, do you?

Audio 1.10

1 Let's go for a walk.
2 I don't like hot chocolate.
3 You always want to win.
4 I imagine that you like swimming.

UNIT 2

Audio 2.01

1 Where were you playing basketball?
2 Who were you speaking to?
3 What was he asking you?
4 Who were they talking about?
5 Why was he getting a bus?
6 What was she doing early this morning?

Audio 2.02

A: I just watched a lovely video.
B: Oh yeah, what about?
A: A man - I think his name was Dean Nicholson. Anyway, he was living in Dunbar in Scotland, but he was bored of working nine to five every day, so he left his job, got on his bike and travelled to Amsterdam, with plans to go to many more places.
B: Good for him!
A: Yes! He travelled through Belgium, Italy and Greece, I think.
B: Very nice!
A: One day, Dean was travelling from Bosnia and Herzegovina to Montenegro. He was riding up a hill when he heard a noise behind him, so he stopped. When he looked behind him, he saw a little cat. The cat was running behind the bike. She didn't want to leave Dean, so he put the cat on his bike and took her to a vet's office.
B: Was the cat ill?
A: No. He wanted to know about the cat's owner, but the vet couldn't find any information about the cat, so the man kept her and now they travel around the world together.
B: Really? How lovely!
A: Yes! Dean named the cat Nala. They've travelled to thirty countries together!
B: Really?
A: Yes! But Dean had to change his plans at first because he couldn't take Nala.
B: Was he angry about that?
A: I don't think so. He said that Nala taught him to take his time and do things more slowly. He stops more often these days. Nala likes to go to the woods or visit the beach. Dean doesn't travel anywhere quickly anymore. He feels more relaxed.
B: Can he travel from country to country with a cat?
A: He can now that Nala has a pet passport. She gets all the right medicine, too. There are some places they can't go because you can't always take a cat into hotels, but there are many other places they can go.
B: What a great story that is!
A: Yes. Dean's got a website, but most of his story is in a book he wrote. He's on social media, too.
B: Great! I want to see Nala!

Audio 2.03

1 I just watched a lovely video.
2 The cat was running behind the bike.
3 He stops more often these days.
4 There are some places they can't go.

Audio 2.04

1 What's the name of your hotel?
2 This is the only morning flight.
3 I'd love to fly over the Andes.
4 We have to wait in the departure lounge.
5 My brother is in the arrivals hall.
6 The plane isn't very big.

Audio 2.05

1

A: Oh no! My dad just messaged me. My parents are coming home early!
B: Oh, this place looks terrible. There are dirty cups and things everywhere!
A: I know! I need to clean the whole of the downstairs right now!
B: Do you want me to help you?
A: Yes, please. That would be great.
B: I can do the washing up.
A: OK, thanks. I'll put all these cups in the kitchen. Then I'll go round and make everything look tidy.
B: Sounds good!

2

A: Hello, do you have an appointment?
B: No, well, yes. I've got an appointment to see Dr White for next week, but I need to cancel it.
A: Do you want me to actually cancel it? Or do you want to change it to a different day?
B: Er, I'd still like to see the doctor, so could you change it?
A: Of course. She has a free appointment on the 24th at 4.30 or the 25th at 9.10.
B: Hmm, I can do both of those times.
A: Shall I book the one on the 24th?
B: Yes, please.
A: Do you want me to email you the information?
B: Thank you, but I'm OK. I've made a note on my phone.

3

A: Simon hasn't done his part of the project again.
B: I know. Our tutor isn't going to be happy.
A: Shall I talk to her and tell her what's happening?
B: That's kind of you. But we don't want to create any problems for Simon.
A: But Simon's creating problems for us!
B: I know! Let me talk to him first.
A: OK, that's a great help. Thanks.

AUDIOSCRIPTS

Audio 2.06
1. Do you want me to help you?
2. Yes, please. That would be great.
3. I can do the washing up.
4. I'll put all these cups in the kitchen.
5. Do you want me to cancel it?
6. Shall I book the one on the 24th?
7. Do you want me to email you the information?
8. Thank you, but I'm OK.
9. Shall I talk to her?
10. That's kind of you.
11. Let me talk to him first.
12. OK, that's a great help.

Audio 2.07
1. Let me carry your bags for you.
2. Shall I open a window?
3. I can take you to work.
4. Do you want us to help you?
5. Let me answer the email.
6. I'll hold the door open.

Audio 2.08 and 2.09
A: My sister and her children are coming for dinner tomorrow.
B: Oh, right. Shall I cook some pasta for us all?
A: That would be great.
B: I can make a cake, too.
A: That's good of you. Lucas and Carla love your lemon cake.
B: I know!
A: I can go to the supermarket later and get everything we need.
B: Do you want me to come with you?
A: Thank you, but I'm OK. I don't need to get a lot.
B: Let me come with you. I can carry the bags to the car.
A: OK. That's fine with me!

UNIT 3

Audio 3.01
1. I have to see my manager later.
2. We have to finish our work by 5 p.m.
3. Do I have to go to today's meeting?
4. My friends have to work a lot.
5. Do you have to work in an office?
6. You have to come and see this.

Audio 3.02
brilliant
clever
delicious
equal
exciting
favourite
popular
real

Audio 3.03
A: I love watching films that teach you something.
B: Me too! And TV programmes. I learnt a lot about English history when I watched *The Last Kingdom*.
A: I don't know that programme. What's it about?
B: It's about a man called Uhtred. He lived in England about 1,500 years ago. It's a brilliant show!
A: Who's in it?
B: I don't know any of the actors' names.
A: Was the man – Uhtred – a real person?
B: I don't think so, but King Alfred was in it. He was real.
A: That's the problem when you watch films and TV shows about people in the past. We don't know exactly what was real.
B: That's true, but you can watch something and then read more about it later.
A: I guess.
B: What TV programmes – or films – have taught you something?
A: Er … I found *Hidden Figures* really interesting. It's a film about African American women who worked for NASA in the 1960s. I learnt a lot from that. But I think films teach us more about now than the past.
B: What do you mean?
A: Well, for example, when we watch films, we learn about different types of people. It helps us to understand them. When I saw *Hidden Figures*, I understood those women better.
B: Yeah. And we see people in different situations and understand those situations better, too.
A: Yes! One film taught me what to do if you have a very small kitchen fire.
B: Really?
A: Yeah! That helped me a lot!
B: Well, I'm glad it helped. So, what did I learn from *The Last Kingdom*? Let me see … I guess it was that life wasn't always easy at that time, so it was important to find good friends and work as a team!
A: That was probably the same in the film about the women at NASA!
B: Ha! You know, I always thought films were just for fun, but now I think about it, they're actually very important for children when they're growing up. They teach them life lessons.
A: And adults, too. I watched a film the other day about how life is short and we need to enjoy it.
B: That's a good lesson. What was the film?
A: That new film at the cinema. It was really sad. It made me cry at the end.
B: What? Now I know how the film ends!
A: Oops, sorry.
B: Now I've learnt never to talk to you about films again!

Audio 3.04
1. A TV show taught me to cook.
2. I learnt about cars from TV.
3. We never watch television in the evenings.
4. You have to watch this programme.

Audio 3.05
1
A: I need to water my new plants. Is it OK to use a cup? I'm worried I'll put too much water on them.
B: Have you got a plastic bottle of some kind?
A: Yeah, I've got an empty one here.
B: Perfect! You can make a watering can. First, put some water into the bottle. After that, put the top on the bottle.
A: Right. OK, that's done.
B: Now, take a sharp knife and make some holes in the top of the bottle.
A: Is this right?
B: No, I meant a small hole, like this.
A: Oh right. How many?
B: I don't know, five maybe?
A: OK … two … three … four … five … done!
B: Now hold the bottle upside-down and the water will come out, but not too much of it, so you won't get too much water on the plants.
A: Oh yeah, perfect!

AUDIOSCRIPTS

2
A: Sorry, I'm late. I had a hot shower and then I had to wait for the bathroom mirror to clear so I could see to do my hair.
B: Did you open the window?
A: Yes, but it didn't help much.
B: You should put car wax on it.
A: The window?
B: No, the mirror.
A: What's wax? I don't know that word.
B: It's what you put on a car after you wash it, so it looks nice and shiny.
A: Oh, right.
B: You have to put it on the mirror before your shower. But don't put too much on. Just a little and leave it there for a few minutes. Then, take a dry cloth – maybe an old T-shirt or something – and clean the mirror.
A: What do I need to do after that?
B: Nothing. That's it.
A: Oh, that's easy!
B: It is. The mirror should stay nice and clear for a few showers.
A: Great!

3
A: The children's toys are really dirty. We need to wash them.
B: We can put the plastic toys in the dishwasher.
A: Really?
B: Yeah. Always put them in a bag first, though. You know, the bags we use to put clothes in the washing machine.
A: Oh right, those bags. All right, let me get one and put the toys in … like this?
B: That's right.
A: What now?
B: Put them in the dishwasher. But always take them out before the machine dries the toys.
A: I'm not sure I understand.
B: Take them out after the dishwasher stops washing and before it starts drying. It's better for the toys to dry in the air.
A: OK, I can do that.

Audio 3.06
1 That's all?
2 Is this right
3 Sorry?
4 Like this?
5 What now?
6 OK, what next?

Audio 3.07 and 3.08
A: I'm really hot and thirsty, but I forgot to put the drinks in the fridge. They're not cold.
B: Put them in the freezer with the ice. You can put a paper towel around them, too. They'll get colder faster.
A: A paper towel? I'm not sure I understand.
B: I read about it online. First, take a paper towel and put some water on it so it's wet.
A: Like this?
B: Yes. After that, put it around the drink bottle.
A: All right.
B: Not like that, like this.
A: Oh, right. Done! What next?
B: Put it in with the ice in your freezer and wait.
A: Does it work?
B: I don't know. I've never tried it before!

Audio 3.09
Presenter: With me today is psychologist Dr Pasko to talk about children and memories. Dr Pasko, my first memory is of boarding a flight. It was my first time on a plane and I was really excited. What's your first memory?
Dr Pasko: I was playing with some water in a large bowl outside a green building. I was about three.
Presenter: I think I was four in mine. We don't usually remember our very early memories, do we?
Dr Pasko: No, we don't remember things before we're between two and four years old, but usually it's around three.
Presenter: Why is that?
Dr Pasko: Well, it's interesting. Children of three, four, five – they can remember things from their past well, but when they get older, from around seven, they start to lose those memories. We don't know exactly why. One idea is that our bodies are still growing at that young age.
Presenter: Interesting! So, why do we remember some things and not others?
Dr Pasko: Good question! There are a couple of possible reasons. First, we remember strong feelings. You had a strong positive feeling when you boarded your first flight. Also, we remember things our parents or other family members talk about. I don't know why I remember playing in water! My parents don't remember it either, and I don't think it was particularly exciting!
Presenter: We forget things even when we're adults. What can we do to help us remember things we don't want to forget?
Dr Pasko: We take a lot of photos on our phones. That helps. We can keep a diary. I've got a friend who collects postcards. She writes memories on each one. I think that's a brilliant idea. There's also a memory box. You write down things you want to remember on a piece of paper and put them in the box. Your whole family could do it together and then later, you can read the pieces of paper to remember the things you forgot.
Presenter: Those are great ideas, thanks!

UNIT 4

Audio 4.01
ate – made
been – eaten
caught – bought
done – drunk
driven – written
read – met

Audio 4.02
A: I was on the radio yesterday, Carmen.
B: What? Why was that, Brett?
A: Because I entered a photo competition.
B: You didn't tell me.
A: I didn't tell any of my friends. Or family.
B: Why not?
A: I just sent the photo in and then forgot about it. I didn't expect to win.
B: But did you win?
A: I came second. A woman from Scotland won.
B: Second is still brilliant. What did you win?
A: £250.
B: Wow!

AUDIOSCRIPTS

A: Yes, I want to buy a new camera at the end of the year.
B: That's fantastic. I've never won a competition, in sports or art or anything like that. Well, I won a writing competition when I was seven years old, but that was a very long time ago and I didn't get any money. Can I see the photo?
A: Sure … here.
B: That's amazing. Where did you take it?
A: In Northern Ireland.
B: Oh, lucky you. I've never been there, but I'd love to go. Were you there on holiday?
A: Actually, it was a business trip. It was beautiful. I was really pleased with this photo.
B: How was the radio interview?
A: It was fun! I was worried before, but everyone was nice and it was fine. You can listen to it online if you want.
B: Yes, I'd really like to hear it! I've never been on the radio. Oh, but I have been on TV in the US.
A: In the US? Really? How come?
B: Well, I was a comedy actor for a few years, and I was on a big comedy programme over there.
A: What?
B: Yeah, three million people watched it each week.
A: Wha … I mean … really?
B: No.
A: What?
B: I'm joking. I wasn't an actor.
A: Oh!
B: I was on a local news programme for about seven seconds! I was visiting a friend in the States. We went to the cinema one evening and when we were leaving, someone asked us some questions about the film.
A: Amazing! What questions?
B: I don't remember. Sorry!
A: What was it like when you saw yourself on TV?
B: Strange but fun! We put the news on later and suddenly, there I was. My friend's television was huge. My head looked really big! They didn't show my friend. She wasn't very happy about that.
A: Oh, dear!
B: Have you ever been on TV?
A: No, but maybe one day!

Audio 4.03

1 I didn't tell any of my friends.
2 I didn't expect to win.
3 My friend's television was huge.
4 They didn't show my friend.

Audio 4.04

1 Which is better, the beach or the mountains?
2 Where's the most popular travel destination?
3 Who is funnier, your sister or your brother?
4 What is the cheapest way to travel?

Audio 4.05

A: Sam's moving into his own flat next week. I think we should give him a gift. What can we get him?
B: I've got no idea!
A: What about getting him a video game?
B: I think we need to get him something for his new home. That's what people usually do.
A: Yes, right, of course. So, what shall we get?
B: How about a plant?
A: That's fine with me, but it's not a very exciting idea. We could get him something for the kitchen. How about some mugs?
B: I'm sure he's already got some.
A: Right, but with more mugs, he could use them when he has guests.
B: Maybe, but that's not really a present for him, is it? I know that he isn't a very good cook, but wants to learn how to be one. We could get a book. Something with lots of interesting recipes that he can make.
A: Yes! Where should we look for one?
B: There's a good bookshop in town. Why don't we go there later?
A: Sounds good to me. Oh, I've just had another idea. Why don't we get him a cooking lesson?
B: Oh. Do you think he would like that?
A: Well, we know he wants to learn more about cooking. He loves Italian food. We could get him an Italian food lesson.
B: That's an interesting idea. I'm sure there's a cooking school not too far away.
A: We should speak to Paola. I think she took lessons a few years ago.
B: I've found their website. Look here are the lessons. Ooh, they're a bit expensive.
A: Ouch, yes, that's not cheap. Why don't we ask Evie and Antonio to buy a cooking course with us? Then it's not so expensive.
B: That's a good idea. I'll speak to them later.
A: Brilliant!

Audio 4.06

1 What can we get him?
2 So, what shall we get?
3 That's fine with me, but it's not a very exciting idea.
4 Where should we look for one?
5 Why don't we go there later?
6 Do you think he would like that?
7 Sounds good to me.
8 We should speak to Paola.

Audio 4.07

1 That's fine with me.
2 That sounds really exciting.
3 That's an interesting idea.
4 Great idea!
5 Sounds good to me.

Audio 4.08 and 4.09

A: What shall we buy Kate as a thank you gift?
B: We could get her some flowers.
A: I'm not sure that's a good idea. She's going away in a few days. She won't enjoy them.
B: Oh, right. How about getting her a book?
A: That's fine with me. Or we could get some of that perfume she likes.
B: It's a bit expensive.
A: Yes, you're right. Why don't we buy her a box of chocolates? She loves chocolates!
B: Sounds good to me! I'm happy to go and get some.
A: OK, thanks. You should go to that nice shop in the centre of town. They have great chocolate there.
B: Great idea!

UNIT 5

Audio 5.01

books	this
is	theirs
its	whose
Matt's	yours
ours	
scarf	

AUDIOSCRIPTS

Audio 5.02
1 We don't have a lot of time.
2 I always put a little milk in my tea.
3 Let's go and have some fun!
4 I need a bit of help.
5 There are lots of people here.

Audio 5.03
Slow cities are where people can have a slower life. They can walk or cycle about. There are green places for people to visit. The food in restaurants and supermarkets is often local and organic and people enjoy healthy living. People also care about the culture of the city.

Audio 5.04
A: With me now is Jay Parker who has a blog all about slow living. Jay, you live in New York. Is it possible to have a slow life in a fast city?
B: Yes. It doesn't mean we stop working. Most people can't afford to do that. Even tiny apartments in New York are very expensive to rent. But we can do things differently.
A: You made a big change to your working week last year. Tell us about that.
B: Yes, well, I'm lucky because I have some savings, so I can now work Tuesday to Friday and not Monday to Friday as I did before. I still work from home. I work from eight to six. Those things haven't changed.
A: And how is your free time different with a slow life?
B: I try to make sure I spend my time well. Of course, I still like to check the news online once or twice a day, but mostly, I try to put my phone away and do something that has a goal. Something that's NOT social media!
A: Ha! Slow food is part of a slow life. How are your mealtimes different today than in the past?
B: In the past, my wife and I ate at different times with the TV on. Now, most evenings, we have dinner together at home and chat about our work or our friends. Once a week, we eat without talking. It sounds strange, but it gives us the chance to notice how the food smells and tastes.
A: Nature is also a big part of a slow life. How do you enjoy that?
B: It's not always easy to be around nature in the middle of a city, and we sometimes have to look for it. For example, I run every morning through a park and make sure I pay attention to the trees and plants, but just walking past trees when I want a break from work can make me feel better, too. The important thing is to notice things around me!
A: I grow plants in my apartment. That brings nature into my home.
B: Great idea!
A: Now, imagine I want to start a slow life from tomorrow. What's the first thing I can do?
B: Hmm. Some people might say get up an hour earlier than usual so you have more time, or smile at people you see in the street. But I think it's important to choose goals that are possible. It's better to have one or two goals and complete them by the end of the day, rather than have twenty goals and not finish any of them.
A: Oh, brilliant idea, thanks Jay!

Audio 5.05
1 I still work from home.
2 Once a week, we eat without talking.
3 I run every morning through a park.
4 I grow plants in my apartment.

Audio 5.06
We all want delicious butter with jam in the mornings, but lots of us find it difficult to put cold, hard butter on our bread. Well, here's the answer. It's the Better Butter knife. It's light and comfortable to hold. It's got small holes in it, so it picks up the butter really easily and spreads it across the bread perfectly. But that's not all. It can also cut slices of cheese, so it's a butter knife and a cheese knife. Another good thing about this butter knife is its price. It's just £6.99. I really love my Better Butter knife and you're going to love yours, too. It's something that every kitchen should have.

Audio 5.07
We all need to look after our things but what about when we go to the beach for a swim in the sea? It's not always safe enough to leave your wallet on the beach when you go into the water. So here's a solution if you're looking for something different! It's the Safe and Dry Wallet. It's not just a normal wallet and I'll tell you why. You can put it in water and everything inside – cards, cash and even photos – all stay completely dry. Think about it. You can enjoy going to the beach without worrying about your stuff! The wallet costs just £19.99 and it comes in six different colours.

Audio 5.08 and 5.09
A: Hello. What are you selling today?
B: Hi! Do you have a pet?
A: Yes, I've got a cat.
B: Do you have a problem with pet hair on your clothes?
A: Yes, I do! It's awful!
B: Well, here's the answer. Look at this glove. It's got a brush on one side, so you can brush your pet with it and stop fur getting on your clothes.
A: That's interesting.
B: The best thing about it is that it's easy to use. You just put it on and brush your pet, then give it a quick clean.
A: That sounds good.
B: Another good thing about it is that pets love it. And we know that it's important to look after our pets.
A: Yes, true. Does it come in just one size?
B: No, it comes in three different sizes so it's perfect for big, medium and small pets.
A: Great! I'll take a small one.

Audio 5.10
A: I need a bike for next weekend.
B: Don't you have one?
A: No. I don't cycle very much, but my friends are going on a bike trip and I'd like to go with them.
B: Can you rent one from a shop or something?
A: The only bike shop is ten kilometres away and I've got to get the bike from there to my flat. It's too difficult. It means taking two buses there and then cycling 10 kilometres back.
B: Can't your friends lend you one of their bikes?
A: They'll need theirs next weekend.
B: You could have mine, but I don't have one!
A: Oh, well.
B: What about your neighbours? Can you borrow one from them?
A: I haven't lived in my flat long. I don't really know my neighbours. Maybe there's a social media group – a local one. I can ask if anyone has a spare bike on there that I can borrow.
B: Good idea! People often put things they don't want on social media and offer them for free. Maybe you can find a bike that way.

73

AUDIOSCRIPTS

A: The problem is that I only want the bike for three days. I don't want to keep it. My flat's on the second floor, so I can't keep taking it up and down the stairs. I don't want to leave it out on the street.
B: Hmm, there's an app. I can't remember the name, but you can rent things from people for a day or a few days or just a week.
A: That sounds interesting.
B: You can look for things in your area.
A: That sounds good. Can you find out the name of the app?
B: Yes, I borrowed something through the app last year, so I have an email about it somewhere. I deleted the app because I didn't use it again.
A: What did you borrow?
B: A barbecue. It was a family party we were having. For fifteen people!
A: Was it expensive to borrow the barbecue?
B: No, it was quite cheap really.
A: Can you lend things to people, too, using the app?
B: Yes! People pay money to rent things from you. So, you could put things you don't use on there.
A: Interesting. I could make some money.
B: Yes, you could. Maybe enough for a weekend away. It depends on what you lend.
A: Yeah. I might give it a try. I've got a few things that I keep thinking about throwing away, but they're still working.
B: Like what?
A: I've got an electric guitar and a really good camera. I don't use them, but other people might.
B: Definitely!

UNIT 6

Audio 6.01
1 I can run quite fast.
2 I don't do it very well.
3 We go there quite often.
4 She does it really brilliantly.
5 We need to move it carefully.

Audio 6.02
1 Have you finished with your glass?
2 We haven't seen this film yet.
3 Has she had breakfast? Yes, she has.
4 He hasn't finished work yet.
5 Has Benji had an argument with Gio?
6 Have we moved yet? No, we haven't.

Audio 6.03
A: I've had the worst day today.
B: Oh no, what happened?
A: What didn't happen? Anything that could go wrong did go wrong!
B: Like what?
A: Well, it started when I didn't hear my alarm, so I didn't wake up until 8 o'clock. I needed to be at work at nine for an important meeting and it takes me forty-five minutes to get to work.
B: Oh dear. Did you get there on time?
A: No. I got dressed very fast, brushed my teeth and ran out of the house at ten past eight! But there were more problems.
B: Oh?
A: Yes. First, I left my phone at home, so I couldn't call work to tell them I might be late. Then, I missed one bus and I needed to wait seven minutes for the next bus.
B: That's bad luck.
A: Yes. The bus journey and the traffic were fine, but I dropped my bag and everything fell out. I was so busy putting everything back into my bag that I missed my stop. I had to get off at the next stop and walk back.
B: I know I shouldn't laugh, but it's quite funny.
A: Thanks! I'm glad my terrible morning has made you laugh!
B: What time did you get to work?
A: I didn't.
B: What? Why not?
A: Well, I was walking very fast to my office when I walked into a man on a bike. He was cycling down the road and I didn't see him.
B: Oh no! Was he OK?
A: He fell off his bike, but he was fine.
B: Thank goodness! But what about you? Were you OK?
A: Not really. I hurt my foot and I couldn't walk.
B: Oh no!
A: I got a taxi and went to hospital because my foot was really painful. I waited for an hour to see the doctor and then another hour before I could leave. I haven't broken anything, but I can't stand on my foot.
B: So, you went home?
A: Yes. I got here at half past one. And I found my phone. I had fourteen messages from my manager. She wanted to know where I was. Each new message was angrier and angrier! I called her and she said she wasn't happy, but I explained the situation and she was fine.
B: Well, that's good.
A: Yes.
B: Well, I can see why it was a terrible day, but you should look on the positive side.
A: What do you mean?
B: You didn't lose your phone. Your manager isn't angry with you. The cyclist wasn't hurt. And you're not in hospital with a broken foot! So, it wasn't so terrible.
A: Er, I guess!

Audio 6.04
1 I've had the worst day today.
2 Did you get there on time?
3 What time did you get to work?
4 I got there at half past one.

Audio 6.05
A: How can I help you?
B: I don't feel very well.
A: Could you tell me your symptoms?
B: Yes, I've got a sore throat and I can't stop coughing. I feel really tired and dizzy and my body aches. I think I've got a temperature, too.
A: When did these symptoms start?
B: About two days ago.
A: It sounds like you've got a virus. Let me look at your throat. Say 'Ah!'
B: Ah!
A: It looks OK there. But you've got a high temperature. I think it is a virus. You should stay home.
B: OK.
A: Take some painkillers. That can help, but you mustn't take more than eight tablets every twenty-four hours.
B: That's fine. I've got some at home.
A: Drinks lots of water and sleep. If you don't feel better in five days, give me a call.

Audio 6.06
1 I've got a stiff neck.
2 I've hurt my shoulder.
3 I've put ice on it.

AUDIOSCRIPTS

4 I'm worried about my elbow.
5 You shouldn't go to work.
6 If you don't feel better soon, give me a call.

Audio 6.07 and 6.08

Doctor: What can I do for you?
Patient: I'm worried about my wrist. I fell off a wall this morning. My wrist is really painful now. I can't move it.
Doctor: Let's have a look.
Patient: I've put ice on it and taken some painkillers, but it still hurts a lot.
Doctor: It's possible that you've broken it. You should get an X-ray.
Patient: Oh no! It's my writing hand, too.

UNIT 7

Audio 7.01

1 Let's see a film.
2 I'd like to go for a coffee
3 Can we go on a bus tour?
4 We need to go to a market.
5 Shall we see a show?

Audio 7.02

1

Marcus: Hi, Jake.
Jake: Oh, hi Marcus.
Marcus: What are you doing this afternoon?
Jake: I'm going out. It's my niece's 6th birthday. She's having a party.
Marcus: Oh, where?
Jake: At a play centre somewhere in town. You know, they have lots of games there and ball pools for the children to jump in.
Marcus: Sounds fun. I'm sure you'll love it!
Jake: Ha! I'm going for the cake! And after all my niece's friends have gone home, we're going to a restaurant for a family meal.
Marcus: Where are you going?
Jake: A French restaurant. I can't remember the name, but people say the food is delicious.

2

Marcus: Zara, are you doing anything tonight?
Zara: Yes, I am, why?
Marcus: No reason. I was just wondering.
Zara: I'm going out with colleagues from work. We're going to the theatre to see a show.
Marcus: Which one?
Zara: Hamilton. I've always wanted to see it.
Marcus: Oh, I've heard it's good. Is there anyone famous in it?
Zara: I'm not sure. I haven't looked up who the actors are. I'm only going for the music.

3

Marcus: What are your plans for tonight, Flavia?
Flavia: I'm going shopping with my sister.
Marcus: Shopping? On a Friday night?
Flavia: Yes, we're going to a wedding tomorrow and we need dresses to wear fast!
Marcus: Are there shops open on a Friday night?
Flavia: Yeah, there's a shopping centre that's open until late.
Marcus: What's it called?
Flavia: The Grand Shopping Centre. It's north of the city.
Marcus: Hmm, never heard of it!
Flavia: I haven't been there before, so I'm interested to see it. It's about an hour away, so it's not close.

4

Marcus: Jimi, what are you doing later?
Jimi: I'm having a night in with Emi. She's not feeling very well. I said I'd stay in and look after her.
Marcus: Oh dear, what's wrong with her? I hope it's not the flu.
Jimi: I think it's just a cold. She's got a sore throat and a cough.
Marcus: That's too bad.
Jimi: I'm going to make her some soup. Then we'll probably just sit and watch TV for a bit.
Marcus: That big new crime series is starting today. You know, the one that's set in a bank.
Jimi: Is that today? Oh great! I've been looking forward to it.
Marcus: Yes, me too.
Jimi: So, what are you doing tonight?

Audio 7.03

1 I'm going out with colleagues from work.
2 I'm going shopping with my sister.
3 She's not feeling very well.
4 I'm going to make her some soup.

Audio 7.04

1 Is there anything nice to eat in the kitchen?
2 There's nowhere comfortable for me to sit.
3 I don't have anything interesting to do tomorrow.
4 I'm bored. I need something fun to do.
5 There's no one strong enough to help me lift these boxes.

Audio 7.05

1

A: Excuse me, is it OK if I take a photo in here?
B: I'm sorry, you can't. You can take photos anywhere in the museum except in this room.
A: OK, thank you.

2

A: Is it all right if we discuss our project in here?
B: Sure, no problem, but you shouldn't talk loudly. People are trying to work in here.
A: Oh, OK. Well, can we use that room over there instead?
B: I'm afraid that's not possible. Someone is using it.
A: That's fine. We'll stay here, but we'll be quiet.

3

A: May I come in?
B: I'm afraid not. We're still having our meeting in here. Can you come back in half an hour?
A: Yes, of course.

4

A: You can help yourself to food in the fridge while you're staying with us.
B: Great, thanks.
A: Just one thing. You mustn't eat Jack's yoghurts. He gets very angry if people do that!

Audio 7.06

1 Excuse me, is it OK if I take a photo in here?
2 I'm sorry, you can't.
3 Is it all right if we discuss our project in here?
4 Sure, no problem, but you shouldn't talk loudly.
5 Well, can we use that room over there instead?
6 I'm afraid that's not possible.
7 May I come in?
8 I'm afraid not.
9 You can help yourself to food in the fridge while you're staying with us.
10 You mustn't eat Jack's yoghurts.

75

AUDIOSCRIPTS

Audio 7.07
1 Is it all right if we wait here for a while?
2 Do you think I could borrow some money for lunch?
3 May I ask you a question?
4 Go right ahead.
5 Please feel free to message me at any time.
6 I have to say no. I'm sorry.

Audio 7.08 and 7.09
A: Hello!
B: Hello. Is it OK if I sit on the floor here? I'd like to draw a copy of the painting there.
A: I'm afraid that's not possible. People walk through here. They might fall over you.
B: Right. Well, may I sit on that chair over there?
A: I'm sorry, you can't. It's actually a 200-year-old chair. You can sit on my chair here. I'm happy to stand for a bit.
B: That's kind of you, thanks. Do you think I could move it over there?
A: Sure, no problem. You shouldn't take too long to draw your picture, though. The museum closes in forty minutes.
B: That's fine. I draw fast!

Audio 7.10
A: Today on 'A photo that changed my life', I'm talking to Aiden Jackson. Aiden, what photo changed your life?
B: It was a photo of Iceland at night, with a beautiful mountain in the background and a waterfall in front of it. But what was special were the amazing green and purple lights in the sky. It was the first time I saw the Northern Lights.
A: Where did you see the photo?
B: These days, we see photos like this on websites or our friend's social media, but this was the 1990s not the 2020s. I saw it in a travel magazine and I knew immediately that I had to go to Iceland.
A: And you got there.
B: I did! I wanted to go when I was eighteen, but the birthday money I got from my parents wasn't enough. I had to work and save for five years first, so I could spend a few months there.
A: And how did you feel when you finally got to Iceland?
B: Excited in the weeks before and then nervous on the plane because it was my first time flying. But once I arrived in Iceland, I was just really relaxed and happy.
A: And you're still in Iceland twenty years later.
B: I am! I found a job I love – not through a job advertisement or friend. I went on a tour of the island and got talking to one of the staff at the tour company. They were looking for another tour guide. I said I was interested and they gave me a chance!
A: Do you still work there now?
B: No, about twelve years ago, me and one of the other guys there, we started our own tour company. We're not rich but we love our job!
A: How often do you see your family?
B: My parents and sister come and visit me once a year. I go and visit them once a year. Plus, we talk online maybe three times a week. I miss them, but I love being here in Iceland. It's where I belong.
A: So, the photo really did change your life.
B: Absolutely!

Audio 7.11
1 I saw it in a travel magazine.
2 They were looking for another tour gu
3 We're not rich but we love our jobs!
4 I go and visit them once a year.

UNIT 8

Audio 8.01
1 Everyone in the world will have a smart phone.
2 He'll be here a bit later.
3 Summer temperatures will get hotter.
4 It won't get any worse.
5 People won't have better phones.
6 I'm sure you'll feel better tomorrow.

Audio 8.02
1 I'll come out tonight if I'm not too tired.
2 If it's wet tomorrow, we won't go out.
3 I don't want to get a taxi if it's expensive.
4 I'll see you tomorrow if I can.
5 If I'm free later, I'll let you know.
6 If it's hot, we'll go to the beach.

Audio 8.03
I have a friend. Her name is Karen and we both think very differently. I usually look on the bright side of life. She sees the negative side of everything. For example, when she started her business, she expected it to fail. When I started my career, I never thought about failing. I only thought about being successful. So, with me today is Dr Philip Warner to talk about these two different ways of seeing life.

Audio 8.04
Presenter: Dr Warner, I'm an optimist. I'm always positive. My friend is a pessimist. She's often negative. Which one is better?
Dr Warner: Well, many people think it's better to be an optimist because they're usually positive. They think that being a pessimist is a bad thing, because pessimists are negative and always think things will go wrong.
Presenter: And is that true?
Dr Warner: Not exactly.

Audio 8.05
Dr Warner: Optimists are often more relaxed because they don't worry or become stressed like pessimists. So, they're often healthier and they can live longer than pessimists. Optimists also feel motivated to do activities. They really want to do the activities because they believe they can do well in them.
Presenter: And what about pessimists? Are they motivated to do activities?
Dr Warner: Yes! Pessimists are motivated, too. One thing that's different is that pessimists worry that things will go wrong. So, they're more careful. They think about possible dangers and they stop if they think they'll be in a dangerous situation. However, optimists think nothing bad will happen to them, so sometimes they put themselves in a dangerous situation and that's not good.
Presenter: So, pessimists take more care and that's a good thing. Optimists take less care and that can be bad.
Dr Warner: That's right.
Presenter: What happens when things do go wrong?
Dr Warner: Well, a pessimist expects things to go wrong and they prepare for that. So, if something goes wrong, they aren't surprised. But optimists are the opposite. Optimists don't expect anything to go wrong, but when it does, they're shocked. They can't believe it! And this makes them stressed.

AUDIOSCRIPTS

Presenter: So, there are good things and bad things about being a pessimist or an optimist.
Dr Warner: Yes, but also, we're both of these things in different situations.
Presenter: What do you mean?
Dr Warner: Well, in some situations, I'm an optimist. And in other situations, I'm a pessimist. That's the same for all of us. We're not one thing. We can be both things.

Audio 8.06

1
Optimists also feel motivated to do activities. They really want to do the activities because they believe they can do well in them.

2
Pessimists are motivated, too. One thing that's different is that pessimists worry that things will go wrong. So, they're more careful. They think about possible dangers and they stop if they think they'll be in a dangerous situation.

3
Optimists don't expect anything to go wrong, but when it does, they're shocked. They can't believe it! And this makes them stressed.

Audio 8.07

A: You're a vegetarian, aren't you?
B: I am.
A: And you've been one for a long time, haven't you?
B: I have. For about ten years now.
A: Wow. That's a long time.
B: You're not a vegetarian, are you?
A: Actually, I am.
B: Oh really? I thought I saw you eating a burger last month!
A: Yes, I only stopped eating meat two weeks ago.
B: Oh, why's that?
A: I'm trying to be a bit healthier. And I guess it's better for the environment, too.
B: Well, those are good reasons.
A: It's hard, isn't it?
B: What is?
A: Being a vegetarian.
B: Actually, it isn't for me. I stopped eating meat because I just don't like it.
A: Oh, right. I'm finding it hard. Vegetables are so boring! I miss chicken. And burgers!
B: Vegetables are delicious! It depends how you cook them, but if you really miss meat, then maybe you should have some.
A: What? You're not saying 'stop being a vegetarian', are you?
B: Yes, I am.
A: Why?
B: Well, if it's too hard, you'll go back to eating meat in a few weeks. So, you need to try something different, don't you?
A: I guess.
B: So, how about having meat two or three times a week for two months and then having meat just once or twice a week after that? Maybe in the future, you'll stop eating meat altogether.
A: Hmm.
B: And then you won't miss it, will you? Because you won't have meat every day.
A: Yes, maybe you're right.
B: And you'll still be healthier, won't you? Because you'll eat less meat.
A: Hmm. OK, I'll give it a try.

Audio 8.08

1 You're not angry with me, are you?
2 It's time to go, isn't it?
3 He wasn't feeling good, was he?
4 I didn't talk to you yesterday, did I?
5 We'll be OK, won't we?
6 You can fix it, can't you?

Audio 8.09 and 8.10

A: We need to use less energy, don't we?
B: Yes, energy prices are going up, aren't they?
A: So, what shall we do?
B: We can turn down our heating by one degree. That'll help, won't it?
A: And we can remember to turn lights off.
B: Yes, and you can spend less time in the shower. You didn't need to spend ten minutes in there this morning, did you?
A: No, I guess not. I love a hot shower though!
B: Me, too. People talk about a four-minute shower, don't they?
A: Four minutes! How is that enough time?
B: Well, you can turn off the water when you put shampoo in your hair.
A: But it'll be cold, won't it?
B: True, but you'll live!

ANSWER KEY

UNIT 1

Lesson 1A
VOCABULARY
1. 1 a (*Cry* and *join* do not come before *to sleep*.)
   2 b (*Hide* and *pack* cannot come before *a sports club*.)
   3 a (*Waking up* and *hiding* do not come before *for a taxi*.)
   4 c (*Cry* and *wait* can come before *him*, but they need a preposition – *cry over* someone, *wait for* someone.)
   5 a (You can *hide* or *miss* a bag, but it doesn't fit the meaning of the sentence.)
   6 a (When you *hide* something, other people can't find it.)

2A 1 c (*switch the lights on*)
   2 f (*get dressed*)
   3 e (*pack some clothes in a bag*)
   4 d (*do the washing up*)
   5 a (*brush my teeth*)
   6 b (*shut all the windows*)

2B 1 dressed (*get dressed*)
   2 dry (*dry my hair*)
   3 do (*do the washing up*)
   4 away (*put away*)
   5 brush (*brush my teeth*)
   6 shut (*windows*)
   7 lock (*the door*)
   8 switch (*off*)

GRAMMAR
3A 1 b (The question is about two choices, so c is not possible. Option a is not possible as there is no *of* – *what kind of drink*.)
   2 a (The question is asking about time.)
   3 b (This question needs the verb *be*.)
   4 b (The question is asking about things, so a is not possible. Option c is not possible because there is no *of* – *Which sort of*.)
   5 c (This is a *yes/no* question with the verb *live*, so we need the auxiliary verb *do*.)
   6 c (This is a question about distance, so a and b are not possible.)

3B 1 Where (The question is asking about a place.)
   2 is (The question needs *be* with no auxiliary verb.)
   3 of (*what kind of* + noun)
   4 Why (The question is asking about a reason.)
   5 Have (The question uses *have got* – there is no other auxiliary verb.)
   6 do (The question uses *have* and not *have got*, so we need auxiliary verb *do*.)
   7 far (The question is about distance – *how far*.)
   8 Which (The question is asking about two choices.)

PRONUNCIATION
4A 1 F (In *wh-* questions, our intonation falls.)
   2 F (In *wh-* questions, our intonation falls.)
   3 R (In *yes/no* questions, our intonation rises.)
   4 R (In *yes/no* questions, our intonation rises.)
   5 F (In *wh-* questions, our intonation falls.)
   6 R (In *yes/no* questions, our intonation rises.)

READING
5 1 friends (Mark and Hanna became friends last year.)
  2 similar (They experienced many of the same things in their lives.)

6A 1 'They were both born on 26th April.'
   3 'They both went to Newbrook Primary School …'
   5 'they both decided to stay at university for another year to become teachers'
   6 '… both live in West London, in apartments that are on the fifth floor'
   7 'They both enjoy going to museums and art galleries in their free time.'

6B 1 1999 ('Mark was born in 1997 … Hanna was born … two years later')
   2 London ('Mark was born in … London in the UK')
   3 three ('When Hanna was three, her family moved to the UK')
   4 restaurant ('Mark worked in a restaurant')
   5 Glasgow ('Hanna went to Glasgow')
   6 art ('They studied art for three years')
   7 four ('They studied art for three years. Then, they both decided to stay at university for another year …')
   8 fifth ('Today, Mark and Hanna both live in West London, in apartments that are on the fifth floor')
   9 museum ('In fact, they met at a museum')
   10 cousin ('he's also a friend of Hanna's cousin')

6C 1 M (He worked in a restaurant.)
   2 H (She spent time in Amsterdam before university.)
   3 H (She works at an adult education college)
   4 M (He stayed in London to go to university there. Hanna went to Glasgow.)
   5 M (He lives with a friend from university. Hanna already lives alone.)

Lesson 1B
VOCABULARY
1 1 b (This person talks about making a place look good, or clean.)
  2 c (A dancer might work at a theatre).
  3 f (A PA does things for a manager.)
  4 h (A vet works with animals.)
  5 e (A factory worker works for a company that makes things.)
  6 a (Authors write stories.)
  7 d (Dentists help people to have nice smiles.)
  8 g (Tour guides show people around a place.)

2A 1 b (We say *it's someone's job to …*)
   2 a (*Sign* can't come before *pay* or *interview*.)
   3 b (We can't use *job* or *career* after *work in*.)
   4 c (We can't use *do* or *sign* before *my own business*.)
   5 a (*Interview* and *industry* can't be *higher*.)
   6 c (*Me* cannot come after *signed* or *developed*.)

2B 1 industry (*food industry*)
   2 career (refers to different jobs after university)
   3 interviews (*had interviews*)
   4 offered (*offered me a job*)
   5 pay (refers to the pay not being high)
   6 contract (*signed the contract*)
   7 job (*my job was to*)
   8 business (*developing my own*)

GRAMMAR
3A 1 b (*Like* is a state verb and isn't usually used in the continuous form.)
   2 c (This is a present habit.)
   3 a (This is an action happening now.)
   4 c (This is a state verb – it describes an opinion.)

3B 1 Are, working (action happening now)
   2 work (routine)
   3 'm sitting (action happening now)
   4 Are, having (action happening now)
   5 do, make (routine/habit)
   6 are, eating (action happening now)
   7 'm enjoying (action happening now)

ANSWER KEY

8 's having (action happening now)
9 Does, eat (routine/habit)
10 don't have (routine/habit)

PRONUNCIATION
4   1 are you doing
    2 are you sitting
    3 are they talking
    4 are we waiting
    5 are they living

LISTENING
5 People pay a Japanese man called Shoji Morimoto to go out with them, because they don't want to ~~be~~ go alone. It ~~can~~ could be to a restaurant, a party or a wedding. One person even paid him to say goodbye to them at a ~~bus~~ train station when they left Tokyo to ~~travel~~ move to a different city.

6A b ('Brides pay me around £2,000 to be their friend on their special day')

6B 1 T ('Sometimes the bride has a lot of friends, but they're all very quiet and she needs someone who's a bit more exciting')
    2 F ('At some weddings everyone knows that I'm doing a job. At other weddings, they think I'm a friend or maybe a cousin')
    3 F ('I meet the bride a few weeks before the wedding')
    4 T ('I couldn't believe how many brides wanted my help!')
    5 F ('I usually get home feeling very tired!')

6C 1 2,000 ('Brides pay me around £2,000 to be their friend')
    2 arguing ('My job is to stop people from arguing')
    3 five / 5 ('It was five years ago')
    4 shop ('I had a very different job! I worked in a shop')
    5 tired ('I usually get home feeling very tired!')

WRITING
7A 1 a few months ('I'm working as a ski instructor for the winter')
    2 doesn't work ('I start teaching at 9.45 a.m. and finish at 3.30 p.m.')
    3 with others ('I'm living in an apartment with two other teachers')
    4 is ('The apartment's not big')
    5 work ('Are you doing the same job?')

7B 1 d (*Here* in the second sentence refers back to Banff in the first sentence.)
    2 a (*That's because* gives a reason for feeling tired.)

3 c (*One of them* refers back to one of the two other teachers in his apartment.)
4 e (This comes after Jamie asks, 'what are you doing these days?')
5 b (This refers to the questions about home and work and is a common way to end an email.)

7D Sample answer
Hi Jamie,
I'm really pleased that you're having a good time in Banff. It sounds fantastic!
I'm living in Florence, Italy at the moment. I'm working as an English teacher at a summer school for young children. I work from 10 a.m. to 5 p.m. with a two-hour lunch break. I'm very tired when I get home, so I know how you feel about your job!
I'm living on my own. I'm staying in a very old, small apartment, but I love it! The buildings around me are all beautiful and I've made some good friends. We go out and eat and have fun in the evenings. Do you go out much in the evening? Let me know!

Lesson 1C
VOCABULARY
1A 1 confident (The speaker is sure.)
    2 positive (The speaker thinks things go well more often than they go bad.)
    3 afraid (The speaker is afraid of falling.)
    4 pleased (The speaker is happy about getting a new job.)
    5 lonely (The speaker doesn't have anyone to talk to.)
    6 stressed (The speaker has a lot of work to do.)
    7 unhappy (The speaker wasn't happy because their food arrived late.)
    8 interested (The speaker is interested in knowing more about life in Mozambique.)

1B 1 unhappy (There's a problem with the room.)
    2 confident (People don't feel lonely about an exam; they feel interested *in* not *about* an exam.)
    3 afraid (The sport is dangerous.)
    4 lonely (The speaker lives alone and no one visits them.)
    5 interested (The speaker wants to know more about the trees.)
    6 stressed (After *tired and*, we need a negative adjective.)

PRONUNCIATION
2   1 a 2 b 3 b 4 b 5 a 6 b

HOW TO …
3A 1 T ('I'm painting my kitchen')
    2 T ('I'm so tired. I don't think I can finish')
    3 F ('But I missed the meeting. I really wanted to be there')
    4 F ('Can I give the presentation with another student?')

3B 1 looks, Nice
    2 done
    3 it
    4 on
    5 all right
    6 Don't, really
    7 understand
    8 That's

SPEAKING
4A 1 mean   4 that's
    2 think   5 well
    3 worry   6 you'll

Lesson 1D
GRAMMAR
1   1 ~~to develop~~ developing (*enjoy* + *-ing* verb)
    2 ~~makeing~~ making (verbs ending *-e*, change *-e* to *-ing*)
    3 ~~cook~~ cooking (*don't mind* + *-ing* verb)
    4 ~~begining~~ beginning (The stress is on the final syllable, so double the *n*.)
    5 ~~no sleeping~~ not sleeping (*hate* + *not*)
    6 ~~having~~ to have ('*d love* + *to* infinitive)
    7 ~~to helping~~ helping (*don't/doesn't mind* + *-ing* verb)
    8 ~~not like~~ don't like (*don't/doesn't like* = the negative form of *like*)

2   1 dancing (*enjoy* + *-ing* verb)
    2 getting (*love* + *-ing* verb)
    3 getting (*hate* + *-ing* verb)
    4 doing/to do (After *like*, it is also possible to use *to* infinitive when talking about the present.)
    5 to have ('*d like* + *to* + infinitive)
    6 visiting (*enjoy* + *-ing* verb)
    7 travelling/to travel (After *hate*, it is also possible to use *to* infinitive when talking about the present.)
    8 seeing/to see (After *love*, it is also possible to use *to* infinitive when talking about the present.)
    9 saying/to say (After *hate*, it is also possible to use *to* infinitive when talking about the present.)
    10 taking (*don't mind* + *-ing* verb)
    11 to use ('*d hate* + *to* infinitive)
    12 being/to be (After *hate*, it is also possible to use *to* infinitive when talking about the present.)

79

ANSWER KEY

LISTENING

3 Louis's dislikes:
walking ('I hate walking')
hot chocolate ('I don't like hot chocolate')
Monday mornings ('I don't like getting up for work on Mondays')
public swimming pools ('I hate swimming in public swimming pools')
Millie's dislikes:
Sunday evenings ('I don't like Sunday evenings')
baths in summer ('I don't like having baths in the summer')

4   1 cold ('I prefer to stay inside in the warm')
    2 doesn't mind ('I like winning, but I don't mind losing')
    3 arriving at ('I like to get to work early')
    4 early ('waking up late at the weekend is worse')
    5 showers ('I prefer to have a shower')
    6 enjoys ('I love swimming in hotel pools when I'm on holiday')

5   1 Let's go for a walk.
    2 I don't like hot chocolate.
    3 You always want to win.
    4 I imagine that you like swimming.

UNIT 2

Lesson 2A
VOCABULARY

1   1 fur (Cats don't have feathers or a trunk.)
    2 web (Spiders don't have or make shells or wings.)
    3 skin (Elephants don't have feathers or shells.)
    4 trunk (Elephants don't have fur or wings.)
    5 wings (Butterflies don't have shells or make webs.)
    6 shell (Tortoises don't live inside their skin or have trunks.)
    7 feathers (Birds don't make webs; they have tails, but they don't leave them behind.)
    8 tail (Dogs don't have wings; they don't move their skin up and down.)

2   1 dolphin   5 tiger
    2 bee   6 snake
    3 rabbit   7 butterfly
    4 frog   8 wolf

GRAMMAR

3A 1 b (The action was in progress.)
    2 b (These two actions happened in time order, not at the same time.)
    3 a (This is a question about an action in progress.)
    4 c (This comes before the past simple; *while* comes before the past continuous; *what* doesn't fit the meaning.)

3B 1 was walking (an action in progress)
    2 had (a state verb, so used in the simple form)
    3 didn't hear (a state verb so used in the simple form)
    4 made, were walking (the second action was in progress when the first happened)
    5 was crossing, fell (the first action was in progress when the second happened)
    6 found, took (two actions that happened in time order, not at the same time)

3C 1 were you doing (action in progress)
    2 was playing (action in progress)
    3 was walking (action in progress)
    4 heard (action that happened when walking home was in progress)
    5 was lying (action in progress)
    6 did you do (ask about a past finished action)
    7 called (past finished action)
    8 came (past finished action)
    9 spoke (past finished action)
    10 told (past finished action)

PRONUNCIATION

4   1 were you playing
    2 were you speaking
    3 was he asking
    4 were they talking
    5 was he getting
    6 was she doing

LISTENING

5A 1 a ('got on his bike and travelled to Amsterdam')
    2 h ('He travelled through Belgium, Greece and Italy')
    3 c (Dean was travelling from Bosnia and Herzegovina to Montenegro')
    4 e ('He was riding up a hill')
    5 b ('When he looked behind him, he saw a little cat')
    6 g ('and took her to a vet's office')
    7 f ('He can now that Nala has a pet passport')
    8 d ('They've travelled to thirty countries')

5B 1 c ('but he was bored of working nine to five every day')
    2 c ('Dean was travelling from Bosnia and Herzegovina to Montenegro')
    3 b ('he wanted to know about the cat's owner')
    4 a ('Nala taught him to take his time and do things more slowly')
    5 c ('There are some places they can't go, because you can't always take a cat into hotels')
    6 c ('Dean's got a website, but his story is in a book he wrote')

5C 1 I just watched a lovely video.
    2 The cat was running behind the bike.
    3 He stops more often these days.
    4 There are some places they can't go.

WRITING

6A 1 dog ('I was out running when I saw a dog')
    2 house ('in the window of someone's house')
    3 phone ('The owner used his phone to open the front door.')

6B 1 Just then (very soon after the writer saw the dog)
    2 First (This is the first action the writer took.)
    3 Then (This is the next action the writer took.)
    4 Later (the time after the fire service arrived)

6D Sample answer
Last month, my friend Marco and I were walking through a park when we heard a sound. It was coming from above us. We looked up and there was a cat in a tree. It was high and it couldn't get down. First, Marco tried to climb the tree, but he didn't get very far. Next, I tried. I got higher, but it wasn't enough so we called the fire service.
Later, a small fire truck arrived. A firewoman climbed the tree and brought the cat down. I walked over to the cat. Just then, it jumped out of the firewoman's hands and ran off. We never saw it again but I'm sure it was pleased!

Lesson 2B
VOCABULARY

1   1 fly out
    2 change
    3 flight
    4 take off
    5 delay
    6 due to arrive
    7 land
    8 arrival time
    9 made a reservation

2A 1 a (A check-in desk is where you get your boarding passes.)
    2 b (This is where machines check your bags.)
    3 a (This is where you wait to board a plane.)
    4 b (= get on the plane)

ANSWER KEY

5 c (Passport control is where someone checks your passport.)
6 c (This is where people check your luggage for things you shouldn't bring into a country.)

2B
1. Check (*check-in desk*)
2. boarding (*boarding pass*)
3. Security (the place where your bags go through a machine)
4. lounge (*departure lounge*)
5. board (*board a plane*)
6. control (*passport control*)
7. get (*off the plane*)
8. Baggage (*baggage reclaim*)
9. Customs (where they check you're not bringing certain things into the country)
10. Arrivals (where people arrive after taking a flight)

GRAMMAR

3A
1. the seat (the second time the speaker talks about the seat)
2. The flight (talking about a specific flight)
3. time (talking generally about an uncountable noun *time*)
4. the Sahara (a desert)
5. in the morning (fixed phrase *in the morning*)
6. the train station (the speaker and listener know what train station)

3B
1. – (place name)
2. – (talking generally about tourists)
3. the (name of a sea)
4. the (both the writer and reader understand which car)
5. the (both the writer and reader understand which map)
6. – (talking generally about different choices)
7. the (both the writer and reader understand it's the road they are on)
8. The (both the writer and reader understand which sea)
9. the (fixed phrase, *in the evening*)
10. – (talking generally about safety)

PRONUNCIATION

4
1. W (before a consonant sound)
2. S (before a vowel sound)
3. S (before a vowel sound)
4. W (before a consonant sound)
5. S (before a vowel sound)
6. W (before a consonant sound)

READING

5
1. C ('I couldn't find my passport')
2. D ('I saw that my purse wasn't in my bag')
3. B ('I couldn't find my phone anywhere')
4. A ('my wedding ring wasn't on my finger')

6A
1. T ('I asked people around me to look for it')
2. F ('she was fine about it')
3. T ('She bought me a new ring when we got home')
4. T ('while I was putting my youngest child in his car seat')
5. F ('I was very upset about it at the time')
6. F ('We went back to the hotel, but it wasn't there')
7. F ('My friends had jobs to go to so they went home')
8. F ('I wasn't pleased, but I felt worse when I got home and found my lost passport at the bottom of my bag')
9. T ('I got off the plane very quickly')
10. T ('After an hour, someone brought me my purse')

6B
1. pool ('I went down to the pool alone')
2. take photos ('I wanted to take photos')
3. husband ('We found it when my husband drove over it')
4. week ('We had a fantastic week in Tijuana')
5. arrivals hall ('In the arrivals halls, I saw that my purse wasn't in my bag')
6. airline desk ('I went to the airline desk and told them the problem')

6C
1. Alice (She put her phone on top of the car.)
2. Lucas (He didn't check his bag carefully and thought his passport was lost.)
3. Emi (She didn't check her seat and left her purse on the plane.)
4. Darius (He's going to leave his wedding ring at home so he doesn't lose it again.)

Lesson 2C
VOCABULARY

1A
1. b (*make a note*)
2. a (*hold the door open for someone*)
3. a (*carry your suitcase*; you *carry* something to another place)
4. c (*hold someone's hand*)
5. b (*take a look*)
6. c (*bring someone some coffee*; *take* means 'to another place')

1B
1. take (*take a break*)
2. cancelled (*cancel an appointment*)
3. answered (*answer emails*)
4. brought (*bring someone something*)
5. carried (*carry a tray*)
6. made (*make appointments*)
7. answered (*answer the phone*)

HOW TO …

2A
1. a ('I need to clean … Do you want me to help you?')
2. b ('Do you want me to actually cancel it? Or do you want to change it to a different day?')
3. a ('Let me talk to him first.')

2B
1. Do you want me to help you?
2. Yes, please. That would be great.
3. I can do the washing up.
4. I'll put all these cups in the kitchen.
5. Do you want me to cancel it?
6. Shall I book the one on the 24th?
7. Do you want me to email you the information?
8. Thank you, but I'm OK.
9. Shall I talk to her?
10. That's kind of you.
11. Let me talk to him first.
12. OK, that's a great help.

PRONUNCIATION

3 2, 3, 5 are polite.

SPEAKING

4B
1. Shall
2. can
3. good
4. go
5. want
6. but
7. Let

Lesson 2D
GRAMMAR

1
1. e (*both* refers to *Nina and Sharif*)
2. b (refers to two of *our friends*)
3. a (*all of us* refers to *the team*)
4. f (*most of them* refers to *flowers*)
5. d (refers to *my friends*)
6. c (refers to one of the children)

2
1. none (*But* tells us it's a negative.)
2. Both (The speaker is the youngest of three people.)
3. them (*Them* refers to the meetings.)
4. you (The speaker is talking to a group of people.)
5. the (This is talking about specific people.)
6. all (*all* comes before the verb.)

READING

3A b (walk away, turn off your phone or computer, do exercise, do something you enjoy, talk to someone)

3B
1. small ('These are not huge problems')
2. sometimes ('It's not always possible of course')
3. turning off phones ('we can switch them off')
4. regularly ('we should all make time for a daily walk in our lives')

ANSWER KEY

5 good ('That's often good for us')
6 talking ('Perhaps the most important thing is to talk to other people about how we feel')
7 don't always ('Talk to friends, family, a doctor or join a club')
8 different ('We just need to find what works for us')

4 1 real ('we can't seem to speak to a real person')
   2 lecture ('We can't always walk out of a … university lecture')
   3 walk ('We should all make time for a daily walk in our lives')
   4 switch ('It can help to switch off stress')
   5 club ('or join a club')

REVIEW 1–2

GRAMMAR

1A 1 How much does this T-shirt cost?
   2 What sort of work do you do?
   3 Where are your parents today?
   4 How far is your house from here?
   5 Do you want to sit here?
   6 Do you have any good ideas?

1B 1 What is your date of birth?
   2 Do you like this song?
   3 How many bikes does Leo have?
   4 Are Tom and Luke brothers?
   5 What kind of videos do you like?
   6 How old is your cat?

2 1 is living (activity happening now)
   2 's working (activity happening around now)
   3 likes (present state)
   4 works (habit)
   5 enjoys (habit)
   6 's playing (activity happening around now)
   7 don't work (routine)

3 1 going/to go (We can use both forms when talking about the present.)
   2 working (don't mind + -ing verb)
   3 to travel (would love + to infinitive)
   4 making (enjoy + -ing verb)
   5 doing/to do (We can use both forms when talking about the present.)
   6 swimming/to swim (We can use both forms when talking about the present.)
   7 to have ('d hate + to + infinitive)
   8 joining/to join (We can use both forms when talking about the present.)

4 1 was eating (action in progress)
   2 woke (action that happened when another action was in progress)
   3 watched (two actions that happened in time order)
   4 when (while comes before the past continuous)
   5 were starting (people = they)
   6 was getting (past continuous = was/were + -ing verb)
   7 went (action that happened when another action was in progress)
   8 was still sleeping (action in progress at a specific past time)

5 1 the (fixed phrase – in the mornings)
   2 the (fixed phrase – in the evenings)
   3 – (talking generally about plants)
   4 – (talking generally about other pets)
   5 the (talking about a specific type)
   6 – (a continent)
   7 – (talking generally about sunlight)
   8 – (talking generally about water)
   9 – (talking generally about tortoises)
   10 the (There is only one ground.)

6 1 b 2 a 3 a 4 a 5 c 6 b

VOCABULARY

7 1 wake   6 put
   2 shut   7 lock
   3 brush   8 dry
   4 pack   9 join
   5 switch   10 miss

8 1 career (talking about a number of jobs)
   2 factory worker (putting things in boxes)
   3 offered (offer someone a job)
   4 job (It was my job)
   5 PA (a personal assistant works for a company manager)
   6 pay (refers to money)
   7 develop (sign isn't possible)
   8 author (someone who writes blog posts)
   9 offered (offer someone a place on a course)

9 1 e 2 d 3 a 4 f 5 b 6 c

10 1 rabbit, rat
   2 bear, wolf
   3 butterfly, fly
   4 bird, chicken
   5 crocodile, whale

11 1 delay
   2 changed
   3 security
   4 boarding passes
   5 landed
   6 departure lounge
   7 baggage reclaim
   8 due to arrive

12 1 Cancel   6 answer
   2 make   7 Answer
   3 Make   8 Bring
   4 carry   9 take
   5 Take

UNIT 3

Lesson 3A

VOCABULARY

1A 1 b   4 b
   2 c   5 a
   3 c   6 b

1B 1 explained (explain something to someone)
   2 plan (plan something better)
   3 describe (describe habits)
   4 search for (search for something online)
   5 Decide (decide on something)
   6 discover (discover something about yourself)
   7 develop (develop a system)
   8 expect (expect something to happen)

2 1 engineering
   2 education
   3 information technology
   4 geography
   5 business studies
   6 politics
   7 medicine
   8 tourism

GRAMMAR

3A 1 c (= it's necessary)
   2 a (= it's prohibited)
   3 b (= it's not necessary)
   4 a (= it's prohibited)

3B 1 have to learn (= it's necessary)
   2 can't copy work (= it's not OK)
   3 doesn't have to help me (= it isn't necessary)
   4 can't use (= it's not OK)
   5 don't have to read this book (= it isn't necessary)
   6 Do we have to do (= Is it necessary?)
   7 can't sit here (= it's not OK)
   8 Do I have to finish (= Is it necessary?)

PRONUNCIATION

4 1 have to see
   2 have to finish
   3 have to go
   4 have to
   5 have to work
   6 have to come

82

ANSWER KEY

READING

5 3 ('Get a book without spending a penny')

6A a book 3 ('It's the perfect place for starting again and spending more time with her favourite hobby of painting. She soon realizes that she made a great decision.')
b book 1 ('she needs to run and hide')
c book 4 ('the Stone family are all together')
d book 2 ('17-year-old Theo')

6B 1 a ('But after one mistake at the airport, now she has a suitcase … that isn't hers')
2 b ('Theo has to decide whether to continue his plan to leave the farm or stay')
3 b (Maribel is alone.)
4 a ('Each person has secrets that no one else knows about – secrets that will change their lives forever.')

6C 1 hotel ('A message in her hotel room'), restaurant ('Can the man she met at a restaurant help her?')
2 lonely ('He's lonely'), sky ('he sees an unusual light in the sky')
3 painting ('spending more time with her favourite hobby of painting'), village ('she decides to move away to a house in a small village by the sea')
4 snow storm ('When a snow storm comes'), secrets ('Each person has secrets that no one else knows about – secrets that will change their lives forever')

Lesson 3B
VOCABULARY

1A 1 b (Only *brilliant* comes after *really*.)
2 c (Only *delicious* describes the taste of food.)
3 b (Only *clever* matches *makes you think*.)
4 a (Only *favourite* follows *My*.)
5 a (Only *exciting* describes the feeling of watching sport.)
6 a (Only *real* goes with *person*.)

1B 1 favourite 5 equal
2 popular 6 exciting
3 real 7 clever
4 brilliant

PRONUNCIATION

2 ●: real
●●: brilliant, clever, equal, favourite
●●●: popular (*brilliant* can also go here)
●●●: delicious, exciting

GRAMMAR

3 1 c (object question)
2 a (subject question)
3 b (object question)
4 a (object question)
5 c (subject question)
6 b (subject question)

4 1 What did you do last night? (object question)
2 Who played the main part? (subject question)
3 Who directed it? (subject question)
4 When did it come out? (object question)
5 Where did you watch it? (object question)
6 Who paid for your laptop? (subject question)
7 What did you think of the film? (object question)

LISTENING

5 b ('I love watching films that teach you something')

6A 1 W ('I learnt a lot about English history when I watched *The Last Kingdom*')
2 M ('It's a film about African American women who worked for NASA')
3 M ('One film taught me what to do if you have a very small kitchen fire')
4 W ('it was important to find good friends and work as a team')
5 M ('It made me cry at the end')

6B 1 T ('King Alfred was in it. He was real')
2 T ('That's the problem … We don't know exactly what was real')
3 F ('I think films teach us more about now than the past')
4 T ('they're actually very important for children when they're growing up')
5 T ('It was really sad. It made me cry at the end')

6C 1 A TV show taught me to cook.
2 I learnt about cars from TV.
3 We never watch television in the evenings.
4 You have to watch this programme.

WRITING

7A A

7B The photo ~~show~~ **shows** an actor in a film studio. ~~he's~~ **He's** wearing a dark suit and a white shirt. There are lights with umbrellas next ~~of~~ **to** him. ~~On~~ **In** front of him, there's a television camera and a man. The man is ~~moveing~~ **moving** the camera. On the left, there's a man and a woman. They're ~~look~~ **looking** at the actor. Behind them, there are some clothes.

8B Sample answer
The photo shows a drama class in a theatre. There are four students and they're practising a play. Two of the students are standing on a box. One of them is acting. He's reaching for something with his right hand. The other students are looking at him. All of the students are holding a book in their hands. Behind the students, there are lots of seats. Above the students, there are some bright lights.

8C Students' own answers

Lesson 3C
VOCABULARY

1A 1 on (put something on the wall)
2 in (put something in the fridge to keep it cold)
3 above (clouds are above a house)
4 outside (leave something outside a building)
5 out of (get out of a building)
6 over (use a bridge to cross a river)
7 inside (keep something inside a cupboard)
8 around (walk around a place)
9 into (go into a building)
10 forwards (move something forwards)

1B 1 a (*beside* needs an object; you can't *stand towards* someone)
2 c (a coffee table cannot be *inside-out* or move *up and down*)
3 c (walk *up and down* a street/road; walk *forwards* to a place)
4 b (we can't jump *altogether* or *inside-out*)
5 b (*from* follows *move away*)
6 a (*forwards* and *up and down* come after *walk*, *run*, *move*, etc.)

HOW TO …

2A 1 c ('You can make a watering can … make some holes in the top of the bottle')
2 a ('You should put car wax on it')
3 b ('We can put the plastic toys in the dishwasher')

2B 1 First 7 don't
2 After that 8 need
3 right 9 Always put
4 meant 10 like
5 word 11 now
6 have 12 sure

PRONUNCIATION

3 1 U 2 U 3 U 4 U 5 D 6 D

ANSWER KEY

SPEAKING

4A
1 understand
2 First
3 Like this
4 After that
5 that
6 this
7 next

Lesson 3D
GRAMMAR

1
1 had to (= it was necessary)
2 couldn't (= it was prohibited)
3 didn't have to (= it wasn't necessary)
4 didn't have to (= it wasn't necessary)
5 couldn't (= it was prohibited)
6 had to (= it was necessary)

2
1 I didn't have to stay late at work yesterday.
2 We couldn't use the road this morning.
3 Did you have to take the bus yesterday?
4 My brother didn't have to go to school today.
5 We didn't have to have our weekly team meeting today.
6 Sandro couldn't answer my messages at school today.
7 Did Alison have to work last week?
8 I had to wear a shirt and jacket at school.
9 Why did you have to work today?
10 We couldn't get a table at the restaurant.

LISTENING

3A b

3B
1 c ('I think I was four in mine')
2 c ('from around seven, they start to lose those memories')
3 a ('You had a strong positive feeling when you boarded your first flight')
4 b ('I think that's a brilliant idea')

3C
1 flight ('my first memory is of boarding a flight')
2 water ('I was playing with some water')
3 bodies ('our bodies are still growing at that young age')
4 exciting ('I don't think it was particularly exciting!')
5 box ('There's also a memory box')

UNIT 4

Lesson 4A
VOCABULARY

1A
1 made
2 ride
3 drunk
4 do
5 had
6 leave
7 run
8 written

1B
1 been
2 seen
3 slept
4 swum
5 met
6 won
7 read
8 bought
9 eaten
10 driven

PRONUNCIATION

2 1 d 2 c 3 a 4 b 5 f 6 e

GRAMMAR

3A
1 c (past participle of *have* in present perfect)
2 a (*ever* is used in questions)
3 b (past simple – we know when)
4 b (past experience with no specific time period; Amara = *she*)
5 a (past simple – we know when)
6 c (past experience with no specific time period)

3B
1 've never done (no specific time)
2 've never been (no specific time)
3 've never seen (no specific time)
4 haven't danced (no specific time)
5 wrote (specific time)
6 've made (no specific time)
7 made (specific time)
8 've ridden (no specific time)
9 rode (specific time)
10 've eaten (no specific time)
11 bought (specific time)
12 liked (specific time)

3C
1 He's gone on a boat trip. (Ryan is still there now)
2 Have you ever been on a fishing trip? (no specific time)
3 No, I haven't (no specific time)
4 I went on one last year. (specific time)
5 I didn't catch any fish. (specific time)
6 I've never done it before. (no specific time)
7 I went camping a lot. (specific time)
8 I've never slept outside.

LISTENING

4A

	Brett	Carmen
been on a radio show	✓	
won a competition	✓	✓
won money	✓	
been to Northern Ireland	✓	
been on television		✓

4B
1 didn't tell ('I didn't tell my friends. Or family')
2 second ('I came second')
3 year ('I want to buy a new camera at the end of the year')
4 writing ('I won a writing competition when I was seven years old')
5 Ireland ('Where did you take it? / In Northern Ireland')
6 news ('I was on a local news programme')
7 doesn't remember ('What questions? … I don't remember')
8 Carmen's friend ('They didn't show my friend. She wasn't very happy')

4C
1 photo ('I entered a photo competition')
2 250 (What did you win? / £250)
3 business ('it was a business trip')
4 cinema ('We went to the cinema one evening and when we were leaving')
5 film ('someone asked us some questions about the film')
6 head ('My friend's television was huge. My head looked really big!')

4D
1 I didn't tell any of my friends.
2 I didn't expect to win.
3 My friend's television was huge.
4 They didn't show my friend.

WRITING

5A
1 Five / 5 ('I ran five kilometres')
2 Fifty-five / 55 ('It took me fifty-five minutes')
3 No ('I never want to run again')

5B
1 Although
2 so
3 but
4 because
5 but

6C Sample answer
About five years ago, I flew a small plane. My partner bought me a lesson because it was my birthday. I love flying planes in video games and I wanted to try and do it in real life. I took a friend with me. He sat in the back and I sat in the front with the pilot. The pilot explained some things to me and then we took off. I flew the plane! It was amazing, although I got travel sick. The plane moved up and down a lot because it was small and I felt really bad. So, I'd love to take another lesson, but I don't think I can.

Lesson 4B
VOCABULARY

1A
1 b (*Quick* doesn't come before *direction* or *travel*.)
2 b (*Air* doesn't come before *trips* or *way*.)

ANSWER KEY

3 a (We talk about a border between one country and another.)
4 c (*Day* doesn't come before *travel* or *journey*.)
5 c (faster route *to a place*)
6 b (Only *journey* comes before *from*.)

1B 1 borders (= the lines between countries)
2 way (*making his way through*)
3 distance (*great distance*)
4 direction (*in the direction of*)
5 travel (*travel industry*)
6 tours (*take people on tours*)
7 journey (*helicopter journey*)

2 1 Sweden is on the border of Norway and Finland.
2 China is on the other side of the world to Brazil.
3 California is on the west coast of the US.
4 Oman is on the other side of the Arabian Sea to India.
5 Istanbul is in the west of Turkey.
6 Paris isn't on the coast.
7 Ethiopia is on the east coast of Africa.
8 You can stop in Nicaragua on your way to Mexico from Ecuador.

GRAMMAR

3A 1 b (With short adjectives ending with a consonant, vowel and consonant, we double the final consonant.)
2 c (To make a superlative with adjectives ending in *-y*, we remove the *-y* and add *-iest*.)
3 a (*the same as*)
4 c (superlative adjective + noun + *to* infinitive)

3B 1 the best (superlative, irregular)
2 the easiest (superlative, adjective ending in *-y* changes to *-y* + *-iest*)
3 cheaper (comparative, short adjective changes to add *-er*)
4 more expensive (comparative, long adjective changes to become *more* + adjective)
5 the safest (superlative, short adjective ending in *-e* changes to add *-st*)
6 more comfortable (comparative, long adjective changes to become *more* + adjective)
7 safer (comparative, short adjective ending in *-e* changes to add *-er*)
8 quicker (comparative, short adjective changes to add *-er*)
9 most interesting (superlative, long adjective changes to become *most* + adjective)

PRONUNCIATION

4 1 <u>Which</u> is <u>better</u>, the <u>beach</u> or the <u>mountains</u>?
2 <u>Where's</u> the most <u>popular</u> <u>travel destination</u>?
3 <u>Who</u> is <u>funnier</u>, your <u>sister</u> or your <u>brother</u>?
4 <u>What</u> is the <u>cheapest</u> <u>way</u> to <u>travel</u>?

READING

5A 1 Iceland ('The Best of Iceland Tour')
2 Seven / 7 ('Spend seven days on this beautiful island')
3 Reykjavik ('Day 1 – Reykjavik … Day 7 – Vik to Reykjavik')

5B 1 F ('look for the Northern Lights in the sky in winter and enjoy the midnight sun in summer')
2 T (It was £1,850 but now it's £1,500)
3 T ('… with breakfast')
4 F ('This does not include your flight to Iceland')
5 T ('Small groups. No more than twelve people per group')
6 T ('Great tour guides')
7 F ('Comfortable bus with free wifi')
8 T ('What do you need to bring? Clothes for warm and cold weather')

5C a Day 3 ('Akureyi is … the biggest town in the north of Iceland')
b Day 5 ('you can see local wildlife')
c Day 2 ('It has some interesting history')
d Day 6 ('you visit Diamond beach with its black sand')
e Day 1 ('Visit the interesting concert hall')
f Day 4 ('visit the baths, with their natural hot water')

Lesson 4C

VOCABULARY

1A 1 a (*get a gift from someone*)
2 a (*unusual* is the opposite of *normal*)
3 c (*get someone a gift*)
4 a (We can't use *low* with *gift*; we need to use *the* before *best gift*.)
5 c (*low* is the only word we use with *price*)
6 b (*receive a gift from someone*.)

1B 1 b (*buy someone a present*)
2 d (*unusual thing*)
3 a (*received a lovely gift*)
4 f (*low price*)
5 e (*get someone a car*)
6 c (*buy something special for someone*)

HOW TO …

2A a video game ('What about getting him a video game?')
mugs ('How about some mugs?')
a book ('We could get a book. Something with lots of interesting recipes that he can make.')
a cooking lesson ('Why don't we get him a cooking lesson?')

2B 1 next week ('Sam's moving into his own flat next week')
2 video games ('What about getting him a video game? / I think we need to get him something for his new home')
3 plant ('How about a plant? / That's fine with me, but it's not a very exciting idea')
4 mugs ('How about some mugs? / I'm sure he's already got some')
5 cook ('I know that he isn't a very good cook, but wants to learn how to be one.')
6 cooking school ('I'm sure there's a cooking school not too far away / I've found their website')

2C 1 What can we ~~getting~~ **get** him?
2 So, what we ~~shall~~ **shall we** get him?
3 That's fine ~~of~~ **with** me, but it's not a very exciting idea.
4 Where ~~we should~~ **should we** look for one?
5 Why don't we ~~going~~ **go** there later?
6 Do you think he would ~~liking~~ **like** that?
7 Sound**s** good to me.
8 We should ~~to~~ speak to Paola.

PRONUNCIATION

3 1 I **2** N **3** I **4** I **5** N

SPEAKING

4A 1 could
2 sure
3 getting
4 fine
5 a bit
6 don't
7 Sounds
8 go
9 idea

Lesson 4D

GRAMMAR

1 1 b (We can't taste or smell cold weather.)
2 c (Sugar doesn't change the smell or feel of tea.)
3 c (We can't 'sound' something in the air; look *at* something in the air.)
4 b (*What does … look like?*)
5 a (We can't smell or feel a noise.)
6 c (*What is … like?*)

2 1 What does it smell like?
2 It smells fresh.

ANSWER KEY

3 It looks nice, too.
4 What does it look like inside?
5 What does it taste like?
6 it tastes good.

READING

3
1 Lancashire hotpot ('There's one dish that always makes me think of home: Lancashire hotpot')
2 Lancashire ('Lancashire is an area in the north west of England, close to Manchester')
3 carrots ('hotpot is a dish with meat, onions, and carrots')

4
1 factory workers ('there were a lot of factories there, and many people in the area worked at them … So they made hot pot')
2 easy to make ('They could put the food in a pot in the oven in the morning and leave it to cook slowly')
3 Not everyone ('many of those people had no oven in their homes')
4 are ('onions, and carrots and slices of potato')
5 isn't ('Everyone makes it a bit differently so there's no single recipe')
6 at weekends ('my parents often made it for Sunday lunch')
7 wasn't ('We had some difficult times')
8 isn't ('they prefer pizza')

REVIEW 3–4

GRAMMAR

1
1 have to start (= it's necessary)
2 have to book (= it's necessary)
3 don't have to wear (= it's not necessary)
4 can't wear (= it's prohibited)
5 can't listen (= it's prohibited)
6 can't eat (= it's prohibited)
7 have to be (= it's necessary)
8 have to introduce (= it's necessary)
9 don't have to bring (= it's not necessary)

2
1 did you live (object question)
2 took you (subject question)
3 cooks (subject question)
4 did you move (object question)
5 does Anna (object question)
6 makes (subject question)

3
1 c (*didn't have to* + infinitive = it was necessary)
2 b (*couldn't* + infinitive = it was prohibited)
3 b (*had to* + infinitive = it was necessary)
4 a (*did* + subject + *have to* + infinitive for a question form)

4
1 have been (past experience, no specific time)
2 has never had (past experience, no specific time)
3 met (finished past event, specific time)
4 has met (past experience, no specific time)
5 Did you enjoy (finished past event, specific time)
6 went (finished past event, specific time)
7 Has he gone (asking about past experience, no specific time)
8 Have you ever seen (past experience, no specific time)

5
1 best
2 from
3 the quietest
4 the most popular
5 the busiest
6 further
7 to
8 quieter
9 more expensive than
10 the most fantastic

6
1 tastes   5 taste
2 look   6 looks
3 feels   7 sounds
4 smells   8 feeling

VOCABULARY

7
1 search   5 plan
2 explain   6 describe
3 discover   7 expect
4 develop   8 decide

8
1 h   3 d   5 b   7 g
2 f   4 e   6 c   8 a

9
1 away from   5 together
2 outside   6 beside
3 above   7 around
4 inside-out   8 onto

10
1 given   6 driven
2 swum   7 caught
3 bought   8 won
4 ridden   9 taught
5 seen   10 drunk

11
1 trip   6 journey
2 way   7 route
3 border   8 distance
4 coast   9 travel
5 side

12
1 received   4 present
2 favourite   5 exciting
3 special   6 get

UNIT 5

Lesson 5A

VOCABULARY

1A 1 c (A *price* can *increase,* but not *cost* or *spend*.)
2 a (A *price* can be *fair*, but not *valuable* or *expensive*.)
3 b (We can *rent* a car, but not *increase* or *offer* a car.)
4 a (We need savings to buy a more expensive item.)
5 a (*a few* + *offers*, but not *money* or *savings*)
6 b (spend *on*, not *in* or *at*)

1B 1 cost   5 offer
   2 spent   6 rent
   3 fair   7 increase
   4 valuable   8 savings

GRAMMAR

2A 1 c (possessive pronoun *yours* = your bag)
2 b (object pronoun *him* = David)
3 a (possessive adjective *our* comes before noun *cake*)
4 c (refers back to 6 p.m.)

2B 1 mine (possessive pronoun *mine* = my wallet)
2 her (object pronoun *her* = Melanie)
3 that (= an old friend giving me flowers)
4 its (possessive adjective for an animal when we don't know the gender)
5 theirs (possessive pronoun *theirs* = my parent's apartment)
6 then (= *this evening*)
7 Who's (*Who is* = question about a person)
8 Mine (possessive pronoun = my house)

2C 1 these/those (= umbrellas, mobile phones, etc.)
2 there (= the Transport for London Lost Property Office)
3 them (= the thousand things that arrive each day)
4 whose (= the person it belongs to)
5 it (= the thing they lost)
6 its (= the lost thing's)
7 them (= the owner – we use *them* because we don't know if the owner is male or female)
8 their (= the owner's – we use *their* because we don't know if the owner is male or female)
9 that (= a hundred years)

PRONUNCIATION

3 /s/ books, its, Matt's, scarf, this
  /z/ is, ours, theirs, whose, yours

READING

4A 1 c ('he found an old video game')
2 a ('They also found a painting there … by the famous Italian artist Caravaggio')
3 d ('Terry Herbert went out … to a farmer's field … found something gold')
4 b ('A British woman bought an old ring … discovered the diamond was real')

ANSWER KEY

4B
1 F ('visiting the house he grew up in')
2 F ('Scott sold it for $9,000 and used the money for a family trip')
3 T ('After five years, the owners learnt that the painting was by …')
4 F ('we don't know who or how much they paid')
5 F ('Herbert and the farmer shared the money')
6 F ('A British woman bought an old ring')

4C
1 gift ('It was probably a gift to him when he was young')
2 400 ('it was over 400 years old')
3 4,000 ('Later, he had more than 4,000 things')
4 neighbour ('The neighbour … asked the woman to check if the ring was valuable')

WRITING

5A c (He found Michael Jordan's old basketball shoe that 'could be worth up to $20,000')

5B
1 there (= the old shopping centre)
2 them (= the basketball shoes)
3 this (= they were the shoes of famous players)
4 them (= the shoes)
5 his (= Michael Jordan's)
6 his (= Michael Jordan's)
7 This (= Jordan wore the shoe early in his career)
8 It (= the shoe)

6C Sample answer
An English man called Paul Raynard was visiting Ballycastle in Northern Ireland with his friend Michael. They were there because Michael wanted to look for his wedding ring. It was lost in a field there. They spent an hour looking for the ring, but they found nothing. Later, they found something, but it wasn't a ring. It was a gold coin. Then, they found another and another. They found eighty-four gold coins! Together, they're worth around $110,000. One coin was very valuable. It's worth around $6,000. The coins are now in a museum in Ulster. Paul and Michael never found Michael's ring.

Lesson 5B

VOCABULARY

1A countable nouns: dollar, hour, jumper, meal, song
uncountable nouns: fashion, food, money, music, time

1B
1 money (*much* + uncountable noun)
2 work (*hour* and *job* need an article before them)
3 social media (*on social media* but *on the news, in a post*)
4 apartment (*a* + countable singular noun)
5 jumper (*a* + countable singular noun)
6 time (*enough* + uncountable noun or plural singular noun)

1C
1 b (*a lot of* + uncountable or plural countable noun)
2 a (We can't use *luggage* after a number.)
3 a (*a* + countable noun)
4 b (*no* + uncountable or plural countable noun)
5 b (*a great* + countable noun)
6 a (*some* + uncountable or plural countable noun)
7 b (*article* needs an article before it)
8 a (*News* doesn't need an article before it as it's speaking about news generally.)
9 a (*a few* + countable plural noun)
10 b (*a bit of* + uncountable noun)

GRAMMAR

2A
1 b (*Aren't* comes before a plural countable noun; c isn't possible with *much*.)
2 a (The meaning of b doesn't fit; we can't use *many* before an uncountable noun.)
3 c (*Many* comes before a countable noun; we don't use *any* in a positive sentence.)
4 b (*too* + adjective; *enough/too much* + uncountable noun)
5 c (*a piece of* + singular countable noun, not plural noun)
6 c (*Too much* isn't possible before a plural countable noun; *too many* doesn't fit the meaning.)
7 b (we need to use *of* after *a bit* and *a lot*.)
8 c (We can use *any* to say that something does not exist.)

2B
1 A lot (*a lot of* + countable noun)
2 Some (*some* + plural countable noun: 'not everyone … some …')
3 no ('boring when … no …')
4 too much (*too much* + uncountable noun)
5 some (*some* + plural countable noun)
6 any (negative verb + *any*)

PRONUNCIATION

3
1 We don't have a lot of time.
2 I always put a little milk in my tea.
3 Let's go and have some fun!
4 I need a bit of help.
5 There are lots of people here.

LISTENING

4 Slow cities are where people can have a slower life. They can walk or cycle ~~around~~ **about**. There are green ~~spaces~~ **places** for people to visit. The food in restaurants and supermarkets is ~~always~~ **often** local and organic and people enjoy healthy ~~eating~~ **living**. People also care about the culture of the city.

5A
1 d ('You made a big change to your working week last year')
2 e ('And how is your free time different with a slow life?')
3 a ('Slow food is part of a slow life')
4 c ('Nature is also a big part of a slow life')
5 b ('What's the first thing I can do?')

5B
1 b ('But we can do things differently')
2 b ('I can now work Tuesday to Friday')
3 a ('I try to put my phone away')
4 c ('Once a week, we eat without talking')
5 b ('I run every morning through a park and make sure I pay attention to the trees and plants')
6 a ('It's better to have one or two goals and complete them by the end of the day, rather than have twenty goals and not finish any of them')

5C
1 rent ('Even tiny apartments in New York are very expensive to rent')
2 Friday ('I can now work Tuesday to Friday')
3 bad ('Something that's NOT social media!')
4 the TV ('In the past, my wife and I ate at different times with the TV on')
5 twenty ('It's better to have one or two goals and complete them by the end of the day, rather than have twenty goals and not finish any of them')

6
1 I still work from home.
2 Once a week, we eat without talking.
3 I run every morning through a park.
4 I grow plants in my apartment.

Lesson 5C

VOCABULARY

1A
1 c (Only a colour is *bright*.)
2 b (Something is difficult to carry when it's heavy.)
3 b (*Heavy* and *thick* don't describe colour.)

87

ANSWER KEY

  4 b (Only *soft* is something you can touch.)
  5 a (*Thick* is the opposite of *thin*.)
  6 b (A street is *narrow* or *wide*.)

1B
1 wet
2 full
3 weak
4 light
5 narrow
6 warm
7 light
8 thin

HOW TO …

2A a

2B
1 us
2 here's
3 got
4 all
5 thing
6 going

2C
1 need
2 enough
3 different
4 normal
5 why
6 can
7 Think
8 comes

PRONUNCIATION

3 We all need to look after our things // but what about when we go to the beach // for a swim in the sea? // It's not always safe enough to leave your wallet on the beach when you go into the water. // So here's a solution // if you're looking for something different! // It's the Safe and Dry Wallet. // It's not just a normal wallet // and I'll tell you why. // You can put it in water // and everything inside // cards, cash and even photos // all stay completely dry. // Think about it. // You can enjoy going to the beach // without worrying about your stuff! // The wallet costs just £19.99 // and it comes in six different colours.

SPEAKING

4A
1 problem
2 answer
3 got
4 best
5 Another
6 know
7 comes
8 perfect

Lesson 5D
GRAMMAR

1A
1 b (*show us her photos* or *show her photos to us*)
2 c (*lend* someone something)
3 a (*buy a car*)
4 c (*left you a note*)

1B 1 d 2 a 3 e 4 b 5 c

1C
1 I offered my spare concert ticket to Simon
2 Did he ask you for it?
3 I sent him a message
4 Shall I give him a call?
5 you want to give the ticket to someone else
6 Tell me a joke
7 I'll buy a joke book for everyone in your family

LISTENING

2A 1 a bike   2 an app

2B
1 shop
2 friends
3 neighbours
4 local
5 barbecue
6 guitar

2C
1 far
2 need
3 know
4 live on the ground floor
5 weekend trip

UNIT 6

Lesson 6A
VOCABULARY

1
1 snooker
2 ice-skating
3 athletics
4 baseball/hockey/cricket
5 bowling
6 rugby
7 scuba diving
8 volleyball

2A
1 b (*go* + sport ending in *ing*)
2 c (*play* + ball sport)
3 a (*do* + other sports)
4 c (*play* + ball sport)
5 a (*do* + other sports)
6 b (*go* + sport ending in *ing*)

2B
1 playing cricket (*play* + ball sport)
2 doing karate (*do* + others sport)
3 going running (*go* + sport ending in *ing*)
4 going windsurfing (*go* + sport ending in *ing*)
5 going skiing (*go* + sport ending in *ing*)
6 going bowling (*go* + sport ending in *ing*)
7 doing exercise (*do* + others sport)

GRAMMAR

3A
1 b (An adverb of frequency comes before the main verb.)
2 c (An adverb of frequency comes after the verb *be*.)
3 b (An adverb of manner comes after a verb and an object.)
4 a (An adjective follows *look*.)

3B
1 I normally go cycling at the weekends.
2 … I don't run very often.
3 When I go running, I run very slowly.
4 I'm often in the pool at the sports centre.
5 I enjoy it, but I don't swim brilliantly.
6 I play badminton badly.
7 I never do sport.
8 … I quite often fall asleep before 9 p.m.
9 I always ride my bike to work.
10 … I have to cycle quite hard.
11 … I go to the sailing club early in the mornings.
12 … I can sail it quite well.

PRONUNCIATION

4
1 I can run quite fast.
2 I don't do it very well.
3 We go there quite often.
4 She does it really brilliantly.
5 We need to move it carefully.

READING

5 A (The picture shows the sports of cricket, baseball and hockey.)

6A should ('I think anyone interested in exercise should give the fourteen free days a try')

6B
2 ('I think this is important because it stops people from wasting money')
3 ('FITNESS@pp has a lot to offer and the cost seems good to me')
4 ('you can feel part of a real class when you're actually at home')
5 ('busy people like me can exercise at any time of the day')
8 ('This app probably isn't for people who just want easy exercise')

6C
1 F ('it's free for fourteen days')
2 F ('There are also hundreds of video lessons to choose from')
3 T ('There are many different types of classes … from yoga to t'ai chi to to using an exercise bike')
4 T ('from ten-minute lessons to sixty-minute ones')
5 F ('This helps you to find the right classes easily')
6 T ('I can't play my own music on my phone and use the app at the same time')

Lesson 6B
VOCABULARY

1 1 e 2 b 3 d 4 a 5 c 6 f

2A
1 c (*pull something open*)
2 a (You don't *point at* or *kick* something to get information.)
3 b (Only *bite* comes before *finger*.)
4 a (*get* something *from* a place)
5 c (Only *point* is followed by *at*.)
6 a (Only *climb* fits with *ladder*.)

2B
1 climb
2 jump
3 kick
4 push
5 fall
6 Click

GRAMMAR

3A
1 a (Only *still* comes before a negative verb.)
2 b (Only *just* comes before a positive verb.)
3 c (Only *yet* comes at the end of a question.)

ANSWER KEY

4 c (Only *recently* comes at the end of a sentence with a positive verb.)
5 a (Only *yet* comes at the end of a sentence with a negative verb.)
6 b (Only *already* comes between a positive auxiliary verb and a main verb.)

3B 1 already got (He did it over a month ago.)
2 just packed (He finished it five minutes ago.)
3 recently booked a company (He did it a week ago.)
4 just given his new address (He did it yesterday.)
5 still hasn't spoken to (He called twice, but they didn't answer.)
6 recently told (He did this nine days ago.)
7 hasn't packed the things in the house yet. (There's no information about doing this.)
8 still hasn't paid (He emailed and is waiting for a reply.)

PRONUNCIATION

4A 1 <u>Have</u> you finished with your glass?
2 We (haven't) seen this film yet.
3 <u>Has</u> she had breakfast? Yes, she (has).
4 He (hasn't) finished work yet.
5 <u>Has</u> Benji had an argument with Gio?
6 <u>Have</u> we moved yet? No, we (haven't).

LISTENING

5A 1 d ('it started when I didn't hear my alarm')
2 c ('I left my phone at home')
3 f ('I missed one bus')
4 e ('I dropped my bag and everything fell out')
5 b ('I walked into a man on a bike')
6 a ('I had fourteen messages from my manager … Each new message was angrier …')

5B 1 8/eight   6 fine
2 teeth   7 taxi
3 8.10   8 2/two
4 7/seven   9 1.30
5 funny   10 14/fourteen

5C 1 stressed (He didn't hear his alarm, so he woke up late.)
2 angry (He had to wait seven minutes for the next one.)
3 worried (He had to wait on his own for an hour before he saw a doctor.)
4 pleased (He was worried it was broken and happy when it wasn't.)
5 unhappy (His manager left fourteen messages that were getting angrier and angrier.)

5D 1 I've had the worst day today.
2 Did you get there on time?
3 What time did you get to work?
4 I got there at half past one.

WRITING

6A a ('I've finally got a car!')
c ('I've … finished my exams')
d ('I've got a summer job in a restaurant')

6B 1 things   5 big
2 hope   6 all
3 recently   7 for me
4 just   8 best

7C Sample answer
Hi Maya,
Thanks for your email. It was great to hear all your news. Well done on getting a car and a job! Not a lot has happened here recently. I've been really busy with work. The big thing is that I have a new hobby. I've joined an art class. It's for people who are new to art like me. It's a lot of fun. I've made a new friend, too. She's the same age as me and she lives in the same town. We went for coffee after the class and chatted for two hours. We're meeting for coffee again next week.
Say hello to Ben and Dennis for me. I miss them!
Talk soon,
Drew

Lesson 6C

VOCABULARY

1 1 emergency   5 treatment
2 medical   6 results
3 symptoms   7 prescription
4 surgery   8 virus

2A 1 b (A person's tongue is in their mouth.)
2 a (A stiff neck stops you moving your head.)
3 c (We wear a watch on our wrist.)
4 b (A finger is on a person's hand.)
5 b (We wear a bag on our shoulder.)
6 a (A painful ankle stops us walking.)

2B 1 toothache
2 painful elbow
3 headache
4 sore throat
5 backache
6 temperature

HOW TO …

3A virus

3B 1 How can I help you?
2 I've got a sore throat and I can't stop coughing.
3 I feel really tired and dizzy, and my body aches.
4 I've got a temperature, too.
5 When did these symptoms start?
6 It sounds like you've got a virus.
7 You should stay home.
8 You mustn't take more than eight tablets every twenty-four hours.

PRONUNCIATION

4 1, 3, 4 (There is a *-t* or *-d* sound before a vowel sound.)

SPEAKING

5A 1 worried   4 taken
2 painful   5 should
3 put

Lesson 6D

GRAMMAR

1A 1 c (adjective + *to* infinitive)
2 c (adjective + *to* infinitive)
3 b (for + someone + *to* infinitive)
4 b (adjective + *not to* + infinitive)

1B 1 not to work
2 of you to call
3 not to get
4 to see
5 of you to help
6 safer to drive

READING

2A 1 brother ('The brother and sister are … two of the youngest people to have flown solo around the world')
2 August ('She left Belgium in August 2021')
3 60/sixty ('Her trip involved sixty stops')
4 January ('and returned in January 2022')
5 March ('…, Mack, left Sofia in Bulgaria in March 2022')
6 August ('and landed in the same place in August')
7 52/fifty-two ('He travelled across fifty-two countries and two oceans')

2B 1 M ('The brother and sister are Belgian … Zara's seventeen-year-old brother, Mack, left Sofia in Bulgaria')
2 Z ('she was the most worried about flying across some of the coldest parts of the world')
3 Z ('took two months longer than she wanted because of stormy weather')
4 M ('he slept on an island where nobody lives in the Pacific')
5 Z ('She slept in an airport in Indonesia for two days')
6 M ('Mack spoke to his parents each day')
7 M ('He enjoyed flying over national parks in Kenya')
8 Z ('four planes from the Belgian air force were there to meet her')

ANSWER KEY

REVIEW 5–6

GRAMMAR

1A 1 yours   4 he
  2 we   5 theirs
  3 hers

1B 1 Whose (question about possession)
  2 its (= the toy)
  3 him (= my brother)
  4 then (= at 6 p.m.)
  5 that (= falling over in class)
  6 mine (= my glass)

2 1 any (We use *any* with a question.)
  2 too much (We don't use *much* with a positive verb; *too many* can't come before an uncountable noun.)
  3 a bit of (*Time* is uncountable so *many* isn't possible; *too much* doesn't fit the meaning.)
  4 enough (*Computers* is a singular plural noun so *a bit of* and *much* aren't possible.)
  5 some (We don't usually use *any* in a positive statement or *enough* after *I'd love*.)
  6 a lot of (*Money* is uncountable so *many* isn't possible; *some* isn't possible in a negative sentence.)
  7 some (We use *some* in requests or offers.)
  8 too (We use *too* before an adjective.)

3 1 Can you show me your new boots?
  2 I've lent Sofia some money.
  3 We've got a leaving card for Zack.
  4 I've passed your email address to Maggie.
  5 Naomi asked me an interesting question.
  6 I sent a short email to all our customers.
  7 Did you tell the woman your name?
  8 Shall I buy some flowers for your mum?

4 1 You don't have to run **fast** around a field. (adverb of manner comes after the verb)
  2 I **normally** go to the gym with a friend twice a week. (adverb of frequency comes before the main verb)
  3 Try to eat **healthily**. (adverb of manner comes after the verb)
  4 It often went **badly**. (adverb of manner comes after the verb)
  5 I was **often** late for meetings and appointments. (adverb of frequency comes after the verb *be*)
  6 I don't **always** have time to do this. (adverb of frequency comes after a negative auxiliary verb)

5 1 Have you booked the meeting room for tomorrow yet?
  2 I've just sent them all an invitation.
  3 Ed has already replied.
  4 he hasn't had any holidays this year yet.
  5 He's already paid for a flight and hotel.
  6 he still hasn't finished last month's report.

6 1 It's hard **to** understand Max sometimes.
  2 It was really nice **of** you to drive me home.
  3 It **is** exciting to think of living in another country.
  4 It was wrong **of** me to get angry – I'm sorry.
  5 It's better **to** get up early than to go to bed late.
  6 Be careful **not** to leave the oven on – you don't want to start a fire.

VOCABULARY

7 1 valuable   5 offers
  2 on   6 increased
  3 rent   7 cost
  4 fair   8 savings

8 1 apartment   6 chair
  2 suggestion   7 suitcase
  3 battery   8 post
  4 jumper   9 lorry
  5 meal   10 word

9 1 narrow   4 plastic
  2 empty   5 soft
  3 bright   6 wet

10 1 played cricket
  2 went skiing
  3 did yoga
  4 played table tennis
  5 did athletics
  6 went sailing

11 1 climbed   6 argument
  2 fell off   7 forgot
  3 crashed   8 took
  4 get   9 dropped
  5 pulled   10 bit

12 1 prescription   4 painful
  2 sore   5 ache
  3 dizzy   6 results

UNIT 7

Lesson 7A
VOCABULARY

1A 1 c (*watch a programme*)
  2 b (*go on a tour*)
  3 b (*have an evening out*)
  4 b (*go to the market*)
  5 a (*see a band*)
  6 c (*go out with friends*)

1B 1 a night in (*have a night in*)
  2 a meal out (*have a meal out*)
  3 a film (*see a film*)
  4 some live music (*see some live music*)
  5 a basketball game (*watch a basketball game*)
  6 some friends round (*have some friends round*)
  7 to the theatre (*go to the theatre*)
  8 for coffee (*go for a coffee*)

PRONUNCIATION

2 1 /j/ 2 /r/ 3 /w/ 4 /w/ 5 /j/

GRAMMAR

3A 1 c (present continuous for future arrangement)
  2 c (*be going to* for a future intention)
  3 b (*will* for a decision made at the moment of speaking)
  4 c (future time phrase – *in a/an …'s time*)

3B 1 going to meet/meeting (future intention or arrangement)
  2 'll get (decision made at the time of speaking)
  3 Shall I (offer)
  4 're going to see/'re seeing (future intention or arrangement)
  5 in (before a time period when talking about the future)

3C 1 'm having (present continuous for future arrangement)
  2 'm going (present continuous for future arrangement)
  3 are you going (present continuous for future arrangement)
  4 're having (present continuous for future arrangement)
  5 're going (present continuous for future arrangement)
  6 'll come (decision made at the time of speaking)
  7 're meeting (present continuous for future arrangement)
  8 Shall I get (offer)
  9 'll get (decision made at the time of speaking)
  10 'll see (decision made at the time of speaking)

LISTENING

4A 1 b (Option a isn't possible because Jake has already said he can't remember the name of the restaurant.)
  2 a (Option b changes the subject. Option a continues the subject of the music.)
  3 a (Option b changes the focus to a different shopping centre. Option a continues the subject of getting to the Grand Shopping Centre.)

ANSWER KEY

4 b (Option b answers Jimi's question. Option a doesn't.)

4B 1 niece's ('It's my niece's 6th birthday')
2 food ('I'm going for the cake!')
3 friends (I'm going out with colleagues from work')
4 hasn't ('I've always wanted to see it')
5 dresses ('we need dresses to wear fast!')
6 sixty ('It's about an hour away')
7 cold ('I think it's just a cold')
8 TV programme ('That big new crime series is starting today')

4C 1 I'm going out with colleagues from work.
2 I'm going shopping with my sister.
3 She's not feeling very well.
4 I'm going to make her some soup.

WRITING

5A 1 are you getting
2 're going
3 're visiting
4 're seeing

5B 1 F (She asks, 'How are you getting from the airport … ?')
2 T ('I've made a few plans for us for Tuesday and Wednesday')
3 F (They are visiting the market. There is no mention of tickets.)
4 F ('the market in the old part of the town')
5 T ('We're going to see a comedy show … It's with local actors')
6 T ('I know you've made some arrangements for Thursday and Friday. Am I included? I hope so.')

6A 1 I'm taking a taxi to Liv's house.
2 We're renting bikes to go to Epson Forest on Thursday morning.
3 We're having a meal out on Thursday evening.
4 I'm going shopping on Friday.

6C Sample answer
Hi Liv,
I can't wait to see you! I'm arriving at 14.15. I've booked a taxi to take me to your house so you don't need to meet me at the airport. The arrangements for Tuesday and Wednesday are perfect. Thank you!
My arrangements for Thursday are for both of us. On Thursday morning, we're renting bikes so we can go to Epson Forest. In the evening, we're going to a new seafood restaurant in the city. On Friday, I'm going shopping. I need to buy a gift for my mum for her birthday. Do you want to come with me? I'd love you to!
See you soon!

Lesson 7B
VOCABULARY

1 1 takeaway
2 used
3 order
4 pick up
5 deliver
6 tip
7 delivery
8 containers

2A 1 a (*a jar of jam*)
2 c (*a bowl of cereal*)
3 a (*a tube of toothpaste*)
4 b (*a box of chocolates*)
5 c (*a mug of tea*)
6 a (*a packet of crisps*)

2B 1 crisps   4 sandwiches
2 butter   5 cake
3 soup

GRAMMAR

3A 1 b (all the people have arrived = *everyone*)
2 a (no place = *nowhere*)
3 c (a thing that wasn't pasta = *something*)
4 c (It's a question, so we use *any*.)
5 b (It's a negative sentence, so we use *any*.)
6 b (*to* infinitive follows an indefinite pronoun)

3B 1 nothing   6 someone
2 something   7 no one
3 anything   8 anyone
4 someone   9 Everywhere
5 anywhere   10 nothing

PRONUNCIATION

4A 1 anything nice
2 nowhere comfortable
3 anything interesting
4 something fun
5 no one strong

4B 1 stressed   2 stressed

READING

5A c (The article describes the good things and the problems of being a delivery rider.)

5B 1 c ('So, it's about good cycling and safety skills, not speed')
2 a ('The delivery company pays me for every order I take from a restaurant or café to a customer. It doesn't pay me for every hour I work')
3 c ('I can just enjoy the sun on my face and the fresh air')
4 b ('it works for me because I love working outdoors and being on my bike for a few days each week. I get to do my hobby while working')

5C 1 Friday ('Between Friday and Sunday evening, I cycle up to 150 km')
2 150 ('I cycle up to 150 km')
3 soup ('When you're carrying soup or hot coffee…')
4 routes ('It's also good to know the area, because then you know all the shorter routes to take and that saves you time')
5 busy ('That's why I work at the weekends. It's always busy')
6 app ('I just use the company's app on my phone to see what orders I have to deliver')
7 customers ('I chat to restaurant workers and customers')
8 sun ('I can enjoy the sun on my face')

Lesson 7C
VOCABULARY

1A 1 a (Only option a makes sense in the sentence.)
2 c (Option a isn't possible because there's no *against* after *lean*. Option b doesn't make sense in the sentence.)
3 b (Only option b make sense in the sentence.)
4 c (Only option c fits the meaning and is followed by a pronoun i.e. *you*.)
5 a (Only option a fits. Options b and c don't come before *on*.)
6 a (Only option a fits the meaning of the sentence.)

1B 1 mustn't touch
2 can't wait
3 don't let you
4 shouldn't lean
5 can't take off

HOW TO …

2A 1 c ('You can take photos anywhere in the museum')
2 a ('Is it all right if we discuss our project in here?')
3 d ('We're still having our meeting in here')
4 b ('while you're staying with us')

2B 1 not fine ('You can take photos anywhere in the museum except in this room')
2 not OK ('I'm afraid that's not possible. Someone is using it')
3 not fine ('May I come in?' / 'I'm afraid not')
4 most ('You can help yourself food in the fridge … You mustn't eat Jack's yoghurts')

ANSWER KEY

2C 1 Excuse me, is it OK **if** I take a photo in here?
2 I'm ~~a~~ sorry, you can't.
3 **Is** it all right if we discuss our project in here?
4 Sure, no problem, but you shouldn't ~~to~~ talk loudly.
5 Well, can we ~~to~~ use that room over there instead?
6 I'm afraid that's **not** possible.
7 May I ~~to~~ come in?
8 I'm afraid **not**.
9 You can ~~to~~ help yourself to food in the fridge while you're staying with us.
10 You ~~do~~ mustn't eat Jack's yoghurts.

PRONUNCIATION
3 1 P 2 N 3 P 4 P 5 P 6 N

SPEAKING
4A 1 OK   5 can
2 afraid   6 think
3 may   7 problem
4 can't   8 shouldn't

Lesson 7D
GRAMMAR
1A 1 b (*in front of*)
2 a (*on the right-hand side*)
3 c (*in the distance*)
4 a (*stand in* a place)
5 c (*in the middle of* a picture)
6 a (*with grey hair*)

1B 1 with (*the man with glasses*)
2 front (*in front of*)
3 with (*the woman with a camera*)
4 without (*people without glasses*)
5 with (*friends with a smile*)

1C 1 Meera and Yu are in the middle of the photo.
2 Yu is in front of Meera.
3 Andre is on the left of the photo.
4 Luca is on the right-hand side of the photo.
5 Meera is at the back of the group of friends.
6 In the background, there is a building.

LISTENING
2A b ('And you're still in Iceland twenty years later')

2B 1 b ('But what was special were the amazing green and purple lights in the sky')
2 c ('I saw it in a travel magazine')
3 a ('I had to work and save for five years first')
4 c ('once I arrived in Iceland, I was just really relaxed and happy')
5 b ('I … got talking to one of the staff at the tour company. They were looking for another tour guide')

6 b ('My parents and sister come and visit me once a year. I go and visit them once a year')

2C 1 I saw it in a travel magazine.
2 They were looking for another tour guide.
3 We're not rich but we love our jobs!
4 I go and visit them once a year.

UNIT 8

Lesson 8A
VOCABULARY
1A become more or better: become fitter, get faster, improve, increase
become less or worse: become cheaper, get smaller, go down
no change: stay the same

1B 1 b (*Up* only follows b, not a or c.)
2 c (*Of* follows c, but not a or b.)
3 c (A person cannot *increase* or *go up*.)
4 b (Options a and c do not fit the sentence meaning.)
5 b (Only b fits the sentence meaning.)
6 a (only a fits the meaning; technology can't increase or go up.)

1C 1 getting better
2 becoming smaller
3 speed of change
4 improving
5 going down
6 staying the same
7 increasing

GRAMMAR
2A 1 b (*will* + infinitive)
2 a (*will* + infinitive)
3 a (*don't think* + subject + *will* + infinitive)
4 c (*Probably* comes between *will* and the infinitive in a positive sentence and before *won't* in a negative sentence.)

2B 1 Perhaps we'll all have
2 We'll wear
3 Will we want
4 'll spend
5 will last
6 don't think we'll have to worry
7 will last

PRONUNCIATION
3 1 will   4 won't
2 'll   5 won't
3 will   6 'll

READING
4A 1 (They both talk about the future use of social robots in business, healthcare, education and for friendship, but they give different examples.)

4B Mentioned in article A:
at events ('When you go to an event … a social robot might welcome you')
in shops ('When you go to … a shop or a shopping centre, a social robot might welcome you')
with older people ('Social robots could play a big part in the lives of some people, particularly older people')
Mentioned in article B:
at office receptions ('When you enter an office building … You might see a social robot')
in museums ('They can also work in museums')
Mentioned in both articles: in hospitals ('Social robots can help busy hospital doctors and nurses / Social robots could talk to patients during their stay in hospital'); with children ('social robots are working with children who have learning difficulties / Social robots can … work with children around the world')

4C 1 room (Article B: 'It might even show you to the room you need')
2 welcome (Article A: 'When you go to … a shop or a shopping centre, a social robot might welcome you')
3 medical history (Article A: 'For example, the robots can find out about a patient's medical history')
4 calm (Article B: Social robots could talk to patients … to help the patients stay calm')
5 worried (Article A: 'They can chat to the patients to help them feel less worried')
6 talk to (Article A: 'The robots teach the children how to talk to other people')
7 studies (Article B: 'They can be a tutor for children who need extra help with their studies')
8 museums (Article B: 'They can also work in museums, teaching visitors … about the things there')
9 lonely (Article A: 'particularly older people who live alone and feel lonely')
10 best friend (Article B: 'twenty percent of them said they think they'll have a robot best friend in the future')

Lesson 8B
VOCABULARY
1 1 + (*hope / good day* = positive)
2 + (*have a dream* = positive)
3 – (*fail* = negative)

ANSWER KEY

   4 + (*have work experience* = positive)
   5 – (*worry* = negative)
   6 + (*bright side* = positive)
   7 – (*impossible* = negative)
   8 – (*the negative side* = negative)

2A 1 c (Only *worry* comes before *about*.)
   2 c (Only *dream* fits the sentence meaning.)
   3 a (*Experience* goes with *work*.)
   4 c (Only *impossible* fits the sentence meaning.)
   5 b (The phrase is *look on the bright side*.)
   6 a (Only *hope* fits the sentence meaning.)

2B 1 dream (*had a dream*)
   2 impossible (*be almost impossible to*)
   3 failed (The business failed after bad decisions.)
   4 negative side (*see the negative side*)
   5 bright side (*look on the bright side*)
   6 experience (*have experience*)
   7 worry (*worry about*)
   8 hope (*hope that something will happen*)

GRAMMAR

3A 1 c (*if* + present simple, *will* + infinitive)
   2 a (*will* + infinitive + *if* + present simple but not with third-person *-s*)
   3 c (*will* + infinitive + *if* + present simple)
   4 c (*If* + *don't/doesn't* + main verb, *will* + infinitive)

3B 1 look (*if* + present simple)
   2 'll see (*will* + infinitive)
   3 talk (*if* + present simple)
   4 'll help (*will* + infinitive)
   5 'll be (*will* + infinitive)
   6 share (*if* + present simple)
   7 won't need (*won't* + infinitive)
   8 move (*if* + present simple)
   9 'll feel (*will* + infinitive)
   10 change (*if* + present simple)
   11 feel (*if* + present simple)
   12 'll sleep (*will* + infinitive)
   13 sleep (*if* + present simple)
   14 'll have (*will* + infinitive)

PRONUNCIATION

4A–B
   2 If‿it's wet   **5** If‿I'm free
   3 if‿it's expensive   **6** If‿it's hot
   4 if‿I can

LISTENING

5A c ('So, with me today is Dr Philip Warner to talk about these two different ways of seeing life')

5B 1 a ('I'm an optimist. I'm always positive')
   2 b ('My friend is a pessimist. She's often negative')

6A c ('We're not one thing. We can be both things')

6B 1 O ('Optimists are often more relaxed')
   2 B ('Optimists also feel motivated to do activities … Pessimists are motivated, too')
   3 P ('pessimists worry things will go wrong. So, they're more careful')
   4 O ('optimists think nothing bad will happen … they put themselves in a dangerous situation')
   5 P ('a pessimist expects things to go wrong')
   6 O ('Optimists don't expect anything to go wrong, but when it does, they're shocked')

6C 1 b ('They really want to do activities')
   2 a ('they stop if they think they'll be in a dangerous situation')
   3 b ('They can't believe it!')

WRITING

7A B (It's talking about Bluebell's dream job.)

7B 1 e **2** b **3** d **4** c **5** a

8A Students' own answers

8B Dear Kenny,
It can be hard when people don't understand how hard you work. If you don't talk to anyone about it, no one will know how you feel. If you stop working so hard, your manager will notice.
Can you talk to your manager about this? If you do that, they'll understand your problem better. You can explain that you have always worked hard, but other people are getting more money or higher positions. Your manager might give you a reason for why you are not in a higher position yet. Or, they might tell you that you will get a higher position soon.

Lesson 8C

VOCABULARY

1A 1 a (A vegetarian doesn't eat meat.)
   2 c (*throw away*)
   3 a (Only *energy* has a price.)
   4 b (Options b and c fit the meaning, but there's no *away* after *throw* so c isn't possible.)
   5 a (We can only *turn down heating*.)
   6 c (We can only use *throw away* with *rubbish*.)

1B 1 pollution
   2 throw them away
   3 recycling
   4 rubbish
   5 heating
   6 energy
   7 vegetarians
   8 environment

HOW TO …

2A 1 vegetarian ('You're a vegetarian, aren't you? / I am')
   2 vegetarian ('You're not a vegetarian, are you? / Actually, I am')
   3 meat ('So, how about having meat two or three times a week for two months')
   4 day ('you won't have meat every day')

2B 1 aren't   **4** are
   2 are   **5** don't
   3 isn't   **6** will

PRONUNCIATION

3 1 N (intonation rose at the end)
   2 S (intonation fell at the end)
   3 S (intonation fell at the end)
   4 N (intonation rose at the end)
   5 S (intonation fell at the end)
   6 N (intonation rose at the end)

SPEAKING

4A 1 don't we (*need* → *don't we?*)
   2 aren't they (*are going up* → *aren't they?*)
   3 won't it (*'ll help* → *won't it?*)
   4 did you (*didn't need* → *did you?*)
   5 don't they (*talk about* → *don't they?*)
   6 can't you (*can* → *can't you?*)
   7 won't it (*it'll be* → *won't it?*)

Lesson 8D

GRAMMAR

1A 1 a **2** b **3** c **4** b **5** c **6** c

1B 1 sunny   **5** powerful
   2 wonderful   **6** sleepy
   3 lucky   **7** sporty
   4 tasty   **8** rainy

READING

2A 2 ('Firstly, technology will be important')
   3 ('This means restaurants won't need so many staff')
   5 ('it's possible that restaurants will be smaller')
   6 ('The menus might look a little different')
   8 ('Our changing weather will change the menus, too')

ANSWER KEY

2B 1 F ('It's hard to know exactly what a restaurant in 2050 will be like')
2 T ('Customers will arrive … then use the phone to order … In some places, that's already what happens')
3 T ('and the staff they have will need new skills')
4 F ('more people will prefer to eat takeaway food at home')
5 T ('we'll all have the technology to tell us what our bodies need. We'll then choose a meal to match that')
6 F ('Restaurants will probably sell more local food')
7 F ('a plant … that can create a delicious high-calorie meal. Not with its fruit, which you can't eat, but with the rest of the plant')
8 T ('We might also see a lot more insect dishes on the menu')

REVIEW 7–8

GRAMMAR

1 1 's having lunch (*Freya* = She + *is* + *ing*)
2 's seeing the dentist (*She + is*)
3 are going for coffee (*Freya and her mum = they + are + ing*)
4 's taking the train (*She + is + -ing*)
5 's going shopping (*She + is + -ing*)
6 're having a meal out; 're meeting (*Freya and Jason* = They + *are + ing*)
7 's having breakfast (*She + is + -ing*)
8 's taking the train (*She + is + -ing*)

2 1 a (question about a person)
2 c (a singular verb follows *everyone*)
3 b (used to talk about no things)
4 c (*to* infinitive follows indefinite pronouns)

3 1 Why is there a car in the middle of the road?
2 My house is on the left-hand side of the street.
3 There's a strange animal in the distance.
4 Who's that woman at the back of the photo?
5 Let's sit at the back of the cinema.
6 Felicity's the girl with the long red hair.
7 I'm the only person in the picture without a hat.
8 I'm waiting for you in front of a lovely old building.

4 1 will life be (question = *will* + subject + infinitive)
2 will probably be (*will* + *probably* + infinitive)
3 won't have (*won't* + infinitive)
4 won't use (*won't* + infinitive)
5 'll probably drive (*will* + *probably* + infinitive)
6 everything will change (*will* + infinitive)
7 'm sure we'll spend ('*m sure* … *will* + infinitive)
8 Will life in 2050 be (questions = *Will* + subject + infinitive)
9 Maybe we'll work (*Maybe* … *will* + infinitive)
10 will be (*will* + infinitive)

5 1 take, won't (*If* + present simple, *will* + infinitive)
2 will ask, needs (*will* + infinitive + *if* + present simple)
3 Will you watch, have (*Will* + infinitive + *if* + present simple)
4 leave, 'll get (*if* + present simple, *will* + infinitive)
5 don't leave, 'll (*if* + present simple, *will* + infinitive)
6 won't, don't study (*will not* + infinitive + *if* + present simple)
7 snows, won't (*if* + present simple, *will not* + infinitive)
8 will sleep, misses (*will* + infinitive + *if* + present simple)

6 1 y   3 y   5 ful   7 ful
    2 ful 4 ful 6 y, y   8 y, y

VOCABULARY

7 1 go   4 go
    2 have   5 watch
    3 see

8 1 takeaway 6 box
    2 order   7 use
    3 carton   8 deliver
    4 bottle   9 pick
    5 pots   10 tip

9 1 mustn't (*mustn't touch*)
2 allow (*doesn't allow*)
3 can't (*can't* + infinitive)
4 let (*don't let me*)
5 've banned (*have banned*)
6 shouldn't (*shouldn't lean*)

10 1 c (*getting smaller*)
2 f (*stays the same*)
3 a (*get faster and faster*)
4 e (*speed of delivery*)
5 g (*The price … is increasing*)
6 h (*your English improves*)
7 d (*The price … has gone down*)
8 b (*becoming warmer*)

11 1 bright (*look on the bright side*)
2 hope (*hope that*)
3 impossible (*be impossible to do something*)
4 dream (*My dream is to …*)
5 fails (*fail* is the opposite of *pass*)
6 side (*see the negative side*)

12 1 environment   5 recycle
    2 pollution   6 heating
    3 rubbish   7 energy
    4 throw   8 vegetarian

CUMULATIVE REVIEW 1–4

GRAMMAR

1 1 Do   4 Which
    2 is   5 How
    3 What   6 many

2 1 'm standing (action happening now)
2 'm spending (action happening now)
3 'm thinking (action happening now)
4 costs (state)
5 love (state)
6 'm feeling (action happening now)

3 1 Sophie loves swim**ming/to swim** in the sea.
2 I really hate **waking** up early.
3 Sonny dislikes play**ing** team sports.
4 Most days, I don't mind **making** dinner.
5 I love begin**n**ing a new notebook.
6 We **don't enjoy** / We enjoy **not** getting up early in the holidays.

4 1 All   4 Some
    2 Most   5 Most
    3 None   6 Some

5 1 have to wear (it's necessary)
2 don't have to leave (it's not necessary)
3 can't wear (it's not OK)
4 don't have to (it's not necessary)

6 1 Have you ever ridden (past experience)
2 haven't (negative short answer about a past experience)
3 rode (past finished action)
4 were (past finished state)
5 's gone (Hannah is at the supermarket now)
6 've never been (past experience)
7 've never seen (past experience)
8 've watched (past experience)
9 Have you ever left (question about past experience)
10 have (positive short answer about a past experience)
11 haven't (negative short answer about a past experience)

VOCABULARY

7 1 dry (*dry your hair*)
2 go (*go to sleep*)
3 do (*do the washing up*)
4 join (*join a gym*)
5 lock (*lock the door*)
6 get (*get dressed*)
7 wait (*wait for a bus*)
8 put (*put something away*)

ANSWER KEY

8
1. feathers
2. wings
3. insect
4. wings
5. skin
6. fox
7. fur
8. tail

9
1. carry (*carry your suitcase*)
2. answer (*answer the phone*)
3. bring (*bring someone a coffee*)
4. cancel (*cancel a meeting*)
5. hold (*hold the door open*)
6. take (*take a break*)
7. make (*make time for something*)

10
1. medicine
2. discover
3. tourism
4. plan
5. expect
6. Politics
7. Drama
8. develop

11
1. outside (*Out of* needs an object after it.)
2. beside (*Together* doesn't have an object after it.)
3. upside down (*Up and down* describes movement, not position.)
4. over (We go *over* a bridge.)
5. forwards (*Move around* doesn't go with *a few steps*.)
6. out of (We can't take something *onto* a bag.)

12
1. trip
2. way
3. border
4. coast
5. journey
6. distance
7. routes
8. travel

HOW TO …

13
1. right
2. understand
3. be
4. Shall
5. can
6. Let
7. help
8. First
9. Like
10. always
11. next
12. can/could
13. don't
14. about
15. fine

CUMULATIVE REVIEW 5–8

GRAMMAR

1
1. no (*No* follows a positive verb.)
2. too many (*Too many* comes before a countable noun.)
3. a little (*A little* comes before an uncountable noun.)
4. too much (*Much* isn't usual in a question with *would you like*; we use *any* or *some*.)
5. many (We say *a coffee* to mean *a cup of coffee*; we use *some* but not *many* before an uncountable noun.)
6. too much (*Too many/much* come before a noun not an adjective.)
7. not enough (*Not enough* doesn't fit the question.)
8. any (*Any* is for questions not statements.)

2
1. I ~~always am~~ **am always** in the office on Fridays. (Adverbs of frequency come after the verb *be*.)
2. They ~~come occasionally~~ **occasionally come** to stay with us. (Adverbs of frequency come before main verbs.)
3. ~~Never~~, Liam and I **never** see each other these days. (Adverbs of frequency come before main verbs.)
4. We **normally** go out ~~normally~~ for a walk in the mornings. (Adverbs of frequency come before main verbs.)
5. Why are you running so ~~fastly~~ **fast**? (*Fast* is an irregular adverb of manner.)
6. I think I can cook **better** ~~good~~ than you. (This sentence needs a comparative adverb.)
7. You sing really ~~good~~ **well**. (*Well* is the adverb of manner; *good* is an adjective.)
8. Something smells ~~strangely~~ **strange** in here. (We use adjectives after sense verbs, like *smell* or *taste*.)

3
1. Have you got Mum a birthday present yet?
2. still haven't got
3. 've already decided
4. haven't had time to look for any tickets yet.
5. 've just had

4
1. 'm meeting (future arrangement)
2. 're going/'re going to go (future arrangement/intention)
3. 're going to take/'re taking (future arrangement/intention)
4. 're going to eat (future intention)
5. 's going/'s going to go (future arrangement/intention)
6. 'll walk (decision made at the time of speaking)
7. 're seeing (future arrangement)
8. is coming/is going to come (future arrangement/intention)

5
1. Is Mariana the girl **with** long dark hair?
2. Use the glass **on** the right-hand side of you.
3. I thought I saw a plane in **the** distance, but it was just a bird!
4. Eric loves lying in the middle **of** his garden with a book.
5. We usually park our car in front **of** our house.
6. I usually sit in the chair **at** the back of the class.

6
1. have (*if* + present simple)
2. don't have (*if* + present simple)
3. will increase (*will* + infinitive)
4. 'll learn (*will* + infinitive)
5. decide (*if* + present simple)
6. 'll have (*will* + infinitive)
7. love (*if* + present simple)
8. 'll enjoy (*will* + infinitive)
9. like (*if* + present simple)
10. will be (*will* + infinitive)
11. like (*if* + present simple)
12. 'll probably love (*will probably* + infinitive)

VOCABULARY

7
1. valuable (describes the clock)
2. cost (an object costs something)
3. savings (*spend savings*)
4. spend (*spend £20*)
5. rent (*rent a bike*)
6. offers (*have offers*)

8
1. baseball, hockey
2. sailing, t'ai chi
3. skiing, volleyball

9
1. toe (A finger is on a hand.)
2. surgery (Doctors work at a hospital or a surgery.)
3. results (*test results*)
4. treatment (No treatment for the broken toe.)
5. prescription (A prescription for medicine.)
6. painkillers (medicine to stop pain)
7. shoulder (*Ankle* is very unlikely!)
8. neck (*stiff neck*)

10
1. have (*have a night in*)
2. watch (*watch a basketball game/TV*)
3. went (*go out with friends*)
4. seen (*see a play*)
5. watch (*watch a race/TV*)
6. go (*go for coffee*)

11
1. hope
2. dream
3. impossible
4. failed
5. bright
6. negative
7. experience
8. worry

12
1. environment
2. recycle
3. rubbish
4. pollution
5. vegetarian

HOW TO …

13
1. all
2. answer
3. got
4. Another
5. best
6. important
7. really
8. yours

14
1. Is it all right for us to use this table?
2. Could I borrow your phone for a minute?
3. Please feel free to help yourself to food.
4. I'm afraid that's not possible.
5. Do you think I could use your toilet?
6. You mustn't talk loudly in here.

CUMULATIVE REVIEW 1–8

GRAMMAR

1
1. was standing, ran (The first action was in progress when the second action happened.)

95

ANSWER KEY

2
2 didn't help, was cooking (The second action was in progress when the first action failed to happen.)
3 got up, was sleeping (The second action was in progress when the first action happened.)
4 didn't do, was studying (The second action was in progress when the first action failed to happen.)
5 were learning, met (The first action was in progress when the second action happened.)
6 wasn't looking, took (The first action was in progress when the second action happened.)

2
1 – (no article before dates)
2 The (It's the second time the advertisement mentions the table.)
3 the (in the evening = set phrase)
4 The (It's the second time the bike is mentioned.)
5 – (no article before a town or city)
6 – (no article before a station name)

3
1 didn't have to (It wasn't necessary.)
2 couldn't (It was prohibited.)
3 had to (It was necessary.)
4 have to (Was it necessary?)
5 didn't have to (It wasn't necessary.)
6 had to (It was necessary.)

4
1 does the film start (object question)
2 makes (subject question)
3 does (subject question)
4 brought (subject question)
5 did you arrive (object question)
6 ate (subject question)

5
1 more interesting
2 the most colourful
3 the most popular
4 the tastiest
5 better
6 the loveliest
7 the most difficult
8 easier

6
1 smells different (everyone = third-person singular)
2 feels hot (spicy food = third-person singular)
3 only tastes good (food = third-person singular)
4 tastes delicious (sweet food = third-person singular)
5 taste bad (food items = third-person plural)
6 smells good (something = third-person singular)

7
1 yours (= your flat)
2 this (this + noun)
3 Whose (question about possession)
4 hers (= her bag)
5 theirs (= their house)
6 its (= its tail)

8
1 for me
2 to buy more
3 some sandwiches for his friends
4 us
5 flowers to your mum/your mum flowers
6 her a card/a card for her
7 her a message

9
1 e (usual for me to + infinitive)
2 a (hard for me to + infinitive
3 d (kind of you to + infinitive
4 f (sorry to hear about + infinitive
5 c (careful not to + infinitive)
6 b (be better to + infinitive)

10
1 anyone (negative question, any person)
2 Everyone (all people)
3 someone (We don't know exactly which person.)
4 everywhere (in every place)
5 anything (negative sentence, any object)
6 somewhere (We don't know exactly where.)
7 nothing (no object)

11
1 'll happen (will + infinitive for predictions)
2 'll have (will + infinitive for predictions)
3 won't talk (will not + infinitive for predictions)
4 'm sure they'll be (be sure ... will + infinitive)
5 'll lose (will + infinitive)
6 'll probably be (will probably + infinitive)

12
1 This curry is too **spicy** for me.
2 You look **wonderful** today.
3 It's not flat where I live – it's **hilly**.
4 It's too **noisy** to work in here.
5 We need to be **careful** not to wake the baby.
6 Thank you, you've been very **helpful**.

HOW TO ...

13
1 were you
2 is it
3 wasn't it
4 will you
5 haven't you
6 can't you

14
1 Shall I make
2 That would be
3 Let me help
4 kind of you
5 want me to carry
6 I'm OK.
7 'm worried about my wrist
8 've broken it
9 whole body aches
10 did these symptoms start
11 sounds like
12 should stay at home

VOCABULARY

1
1 industry
2 job
3 offered
4 personal assistant
5 sign
6 pay
7 career
8 developed

2
1 pleased   4 positive
2 afraid   5 stressed
3 lonely   6 confident

3
1 boarding pass
2 check-in desk
3 passport control
4 security
5 departure lounge
6 board
7 flight
8 delay

4
1 clever   4 real
2 popular   5 delicious
3 equal

5
1 bought   4 won
2 ridden   5 taught
3 read   6 wrote

6
1 get   4 special
2 prices   5 unusual
3 presents   6 receive

7 countable nouns: bag, carrot, meal, message, minute, tip
uncountable nouns: electricity, fashion, furniture, luggage, music, work

8
1 thick, thin   5 strong, weak
2 dark, light   6 plastic, soft
3 metal, plastic   7 dark, empty
4 narrow, wide   8 empty, full

9
1 push
2 have
3 take
4 left
5 get/take, down
6 forget

10 1 c 2 f 3 a 4 e 5 b 6 d

11 1 c 2 d 3 b 4 e 5 a

12
1 get faster   4 speed
2 become   5 down
3 improve   6 the same